Dave's LIFE LINES

Take Two!

*Featuring Motivational Thoughts and Observations
by my Family & Friends*

Written and Collected

By

Dave Willert

Illustrated by Doug Kuhl

"Dave's LIFE LINES, Take Two!" written and collected by Dave Willert. ISBN 978-1-951985-27-1 (hardcover).

Published 2020 by Virtualbookworm.com Publishing Inc., P.O. Box 9949, College Station, TX 77842, US. ©2020, Dave Willert.

DEDICATION

'Dave's Life Lines... Take Two,' is sincerely dedicated to everyone who contributed to its publication, through composing or sharing a motivational thought or observation. It's also dedicated to all of those wonderful people who inspire me daily, through their creative and heartfelt achievements and through the kindnesses they never cease to share. Of these people, I especially wish to thank *Marti Repp, Bill Kuhl, Gene Nobles* and *John South,* for reasons explained at the beginning of each of the following four chapters. In addition, I wish to dedicate this book to 'Renaissance Man Extraordinaire,' *Doug Kuhl.* He illustrated the first volume of this series, *'Dave's Life Lines,'* so perfectly, and his drawings were so well received, that I asked him (*begged him, actually*) to double his output this time around, from twenty to forty, and he of course... agreed! His drawings are once again... *perfection*! I also wish to thank my wife, Margaret, and my son, Alex, who have both been *incredibly supportive* throughout this entire process!

Don't you agree that life is even more wonderful when you are able to create a heartfelt project, participating with such wonderful people? My gratitude goes far beyond words! ***Thank you, with all my heart...*** to everyone involved with this book!

Sincerely,

Dave Willert

TABLE OF CONTENTS

PROLOGUE

Before publishing 'Dave's Life Lines,' last year, I asked myself what the purpose of a book full of motivational sayings was? Who was its target audience? Well, the purpose of 'Dave's Life Lines,' is, as I'm sure you have guessed, to entertain and to help others by sharing 'learned wisdoms' of all sorts. Its target audience is... well, that would be everyone... or no one... or probably some number in-between... depending upon who was actually interested in reading it. Although I was okay with that, I still longed to find a way to make this type of book interesting to a broader audience. About a month after the book's release, it was suggested to me that perhaps my next book should feature a diverse group of literary contributors, who could bring a whole new collaborative attitude to this self-help book concept, and with that... it might appeal to a broader audience? So, I gathered together selected members of my family and friends, who expressed an interest in contributing to this book... and voila! It was magic!

Those wonderful people shared or created mountains of quality material! I feel so blessed to have had this magnificent experience with everyone in the group! Many of their motivational sayings involved topics or viewpoints, I would never have thought to pursue, myself... and that alone brought a striking freshness to this book!

Basically, '*Dave's Life Lines... Take Two,*' is set-up in much the same way as its predecessor, with each saying being placed inside a chapter, according to its appropriate category. Although it's nearly impossible to nail down every saying to only one category... we certainly did our best! This time around, the categories include:

MOTIVATIONAL THOUGHTS!

POSITIVE THOUGHTS!

RANDOM OBSERVATIONS!

In addition, we've added a brand-new category to this book, called **HUMOROUS THOUGHTS**! Many people suggested we include this category for the new book, and I was only too happy to oblige! Humor is a wonderful method of sharing motivational sayings or of just making us laugh. However, I must confess, there are *many* different types of humor in this chapter, so depending on your point of view, some of these sayings may or *may not* be motivational or even funny to you! However, they should all make you chuckle... or at least *groan*... and that, my friends, is the perfect way to finish off a book!

477, of this book's motivational sayings, or over *half* of the *859* in total, were *not* composed by me. They were written or shared, for the most part, by members of my family and friends. I can't thank them enough for being so prolific, and making such an incredible impact on this second volume! I want to thank all *266 literary contributors*, whether they personally *wrote* or *shared* sayings. Most of our contributors were not professional writers or philosophers, themselves, making this book that much more down to earth, and suitable for virtually everyone to read! If you were a contributor to this book, although I was very careful, my apologies to you if I inadvertently left your name off the list of contributors. I have ***highlighted and underlined*** the names of the *100 contributors who are part of my family and friends*. All names of contributors are listed in random order, because I feel that everyone associated with the creation of this book deserves equal importance! A great big thank you, goes out to: Vincent van Gogh, Mo Farrah, **Cheri Martinson, Janae West,** John Wayne, Steven Wright, Mel Brooks, **LuAnne Ponce Montilla,** Gandhi, Robert Braun, **Patricia A. Morris,** Theodore Roosevelt, John F. Kennedy, **Robert Willert,** Stephen Colbert, Napoleon Bonaparte, **Catherine Foley, Wendy Miguel,** Lucille Ball, Helen Hayes, Lao Tzu, Bill Murray, William of Ockham, Alexander Pope, **James Willert, Eddie Sibal, Shun L. Griffin, Lizsa Pinedo, Kevin Pinedo, Julianne Hunt,** Claude-Michel Schonberg, John Cameron, Ziad Adelinour, **Lysa Gamboa-Levy,** Robert Schuler, Martha Beck, Susie Harriger, Elisabeth Kubler-Ross, Walt Disney, Quincy Jones, Benjamin Franklin, Saint Faustina, Magic Johnson, Carl Bard, **Vangie Obrero, Barbara Kovacs-Minar,** Will Ferrell, **Jennifer Zamora,** Jon Bon Jovi, Lord Chesterfield, John Muir, Cynthia Heimel, Nelson Mandela, George MacDonald, **Kathy Walborn, Leticia Garcia,** Kahlil Gibran, Larry Winget, William Shakespeare, Vince Lombardi, Johnny Depp, Socrates, **Elizabeth Garcia,** Dolly Parton, **Annie Accetta-Canet,** Desiderata, Joan Rivers, Betty White, **Margaret Willert, Alex Willert, Katie Willert,** Malcolm X, Bruce Lee, **Carl Nielsen, Melinda Nielsen, Kurt Nielsen, Frances Nielsen,** Jane Wagner, Emo Phillips, Whoopi Goldberg, Germany Kent, Amelia Earhart, Anne Frank, Thomas S. Monson, Percy B. Green, Richelle E. Goodrich, Tony Gaskins, **Susan Elias,** Ricky Gervais, Dr. Seuss, Emily Dickinson, Maya Angelou, Aldous Huxley, Henry Ward Beecher, **Ruth Jane Willert, Kirra Willert, Michelle Willert, Dina Willert, Jon Willert,** Lisa Heckman, Moshe Dayan, Arthur Koestler, Julie Andrews, J. Hawkeye, Ed Mylett, Mary Anne Radmacher, Charles Dickins, **Christi B. Lajoie,** Monty Python, Amo Mama, **Rita Jones,** Alfred Hitchcock, George Burns, Buddy Hacket, George Bernard Shaw, R.J. Palacio, **Samantha Dizon, Laura Isbell, Yolanda Setoodeh,** Laura Vanderkam, Lewis Carroll, Elizabeth Rose, Mandy Hale, Steve Martin, George Carlin, Sean Connery, Kobe Bryant, Frederick Douglass, **Anne Buccola-Wiencek,** Panache Desai, H.W. Longfellow, **Lauren Poling,** Pastor Gene Appel, Brendan Burchard, Ernest Hemingway, Helen Keller, Kurt Vonnegut, Alan Dundes, Clint Eastwood, Alex Haley, Rodney Dangerfield, Billy Connelly, Nancy Leigh DeMoss, S.C. Lourie, **Mike Gash,** Morihei Ueshiba, David Allen, **Patricia Mountain-Romero, Justin Senneff,** Ella Fitzgerald, Omid Safi, **Chris Breyer,** Al Capone, Henry Ford, Anna Clark, Ruth Ann Schabacker, Robin Crow, Tom Robbins, **Jeanette Zapata, Leonel Diaz, Yvette Hernandez,** Phyllis Diller, Woody Allen, **Melanie Bowles-Azpeitia,** Eleanor Roosevelt, Karen Salmansohn, **Vincent Washington,** Lois Mcbride Bujold, **Jerry Halpin, John South, Annie South, Natalia Todorov, Marti Repp, Bill Repp,** Ralph Waldo Emerson, Romeo Rodriguez, Bob Fosse, Joyce Meyer, Maryam Hasnqa, Muhammad Ali, G.K. Chesterton, **Tami Seaton,** Alistair Macleod, **Jenevieve M. Fuentes,** Bobby Schuler, Pamela Cummins, Anna Clarke, **Annette Ambrose-Schumann, Troy Peace, Colleen Caron, Lizabeth Guichard, Sarah Turner, Greg Wells,** Chrissie Casey-Brockman, **Douglas Newton,** Kim Godby, **Marylen Ayash-Borgen, Marcia Holman, Stephen Murray, Keree**

James, Haylie James, Coco James, Milton Berle, Kevin Hart, Cary Grant, Woody Allen, John Tesh, Buddha, **Lori Halopoff-Fenelon,** Plato, **Claire Manson, Yen Mai, Stan Knight, Laura Ann Washington-Franklin, Teresa Cimino,** J.C. Watts, **Sabrina Ganier, Erin Garcia, Tassa Hampton-Varga,** Dawna Marcova, Charles M. Blow, **Cheri Hale-Patterson,** Andy Warhol, **Drea Silva, Kathleen Scott-Kay, Amanda Moh, Gene Nobles, Betty Gardea, Amy Wells, Yolanda Rodriguez, Ruth Ellis,** BF Skinner, Tab D'Biassi, **Linda Atherton, Stephanie Miller, Lawrence Vondrake Fitz,** Danny Kaye, **Debbie Lee, Catherine Rhodes, Carlos Morales,** Mickey Rooney, **Della Long,** A.A. Milne, Will Rogers, Mark Twain, Tom Lehrer, Zig Ziglar, Dalai Lama, Lily Tomlin, Voltaire, Robert Frost, **Melanie Blankenship, Doug Kuhl, Bill Kuhl,** Albert Einstein, Sir Winston Churchill, Charles Schultz, Katina Ferguson, Hyacinth Mottley, Kyle Chandler, Robert Benchley, Charleton Heston, Confucius, Abraham Lincoln, H. L. Mencken and Oscar Wilde.

I also mustn't forget to thank all **38 official members** of the **'Dave's Life Lines… Take Two,'** Facebook group. They have been exceptionally busy and added greatly to this book's varied content and/or were very supportive of each other's contributions. These 38 superstars include:

Margaret Willert, Katie Willert, Catherine Foley, Keree James, Linda Atherton, Stephanie Miller, Jon Willert, Kurt Nielsen, Marti Repp, Gene Nobles, Marcia Holman, Kathy Walborn, Douglas Newton, Claudia Proctor-Newton, Jerry Halpin, Natalia Todorov, Andrea Strom, Anne Buccola-Wiencek, Lauren Poling, Kathleen Scott-Kay, Laura Ann Washington-Franklin, Sabrina Ganier, Vangie Obrero, Erin Garcia, Amy Wells, Teresa Cimino, Lori Halopoff-Fenelon, Tassa Hampton-Varga, Lawrence Vondrake Fitz, Yvette Hernandez, Leonel Diaz, Ernie Tovar, Jeanette Zapata, Wendy Miguel, Richie Miguel, Claire Manson, Samantha Dizon and Sarah Turner.

I asked the members of this group what they had learned as a result of contributing to this book, and I received a plethora of wonderful responses! Some excerpts from these responses include, **K**eree **J**ames, who wrote, "I loved having the opportunity to contribute to this book because I think it's so important for all of us to be able to share any little bit of wisdom, inspiration or humor to add to someone's day!" **D**ouglas **N**ewton added, "Thinking, dreaming, creating, analyzing or finding sayings and reading hundreds submitted by others was a fun, challenging and enlightening exercise." **E**rin **G**arcia, had this to say, "It's been neat to see the patterns that intertwine and connect us all. It's quite evident we all have this shared positivity and hope, for the world." **T**assa **H**ampton-**V**arga shared, "While making my contributions to this book, I was already going through a difficult time. Being a single mom in a foreign country is not fun. But this gave me a reason to find the light in the dark." **G**ene **N**obles said this, "It has been extremely interesting to me to daily see the postings from the people I know. This book is going to belong on all our coffee tables!" **T**eresa **C**imino wrote, "Over the years, I have realized that many bits of wisdom that come out of my mouth are the voices of the people who have taught me the most about being a decent human being." **M**arcia **H**olman noted, "It is wonderful to have a book full of unique, positive motivational sayings that you have combined and now are sharing with many generations!" **J**erry **H**alpin shared, "Creating motivational moments has been a huge part of my life. Over the years I compiled a list of sayings from my days teaching, coaching and running activities. For this book, I shared sayings from that list… sayings that meant a lot to me." According to **S**arah **T**urner, "Dave was my high school choir director, with an unending, positive perspective for life. Even after I graduated, Dave still sought to bring positivity to people in the form of this book! What a good source of light in a dark time!" Lori Halopoff-Fenelon said, "During this process I came to learn which phrases, quotes and mantras have stuck in my mind and influenced me in some way. I think sometimes you can say more substantive concepts with a short phrase, than you can with a full paragraph." Natalia Todorov, had this to say, "I am super thankful and honored to have been invited to be a part of this group. Becoming a member led me to wake up my inner soul, thought juices, which focused me more on the really important things in life." Marti Repp added, "I enjoyed participating in the writing of this book and feel honored to have had you ask me. I didn't partake as much as I should have, I was too busy reading everyone's good writing!" Laura Ann Washington-Franklin wrote, "While contributing to this work of art, it was a joy to add words of encouragement for this generation and the next!" Amy Wells noted, "Thank you for inviting all of us to be a part of your world!" Samantha Dizon shared, "You encouraged me to write and contribute some lines, and I was really excited! I gave one of my favorite quotes and I believe I gave two that I created. Thank you again for this opportunity. I'm honored to be the youngest member of the group!" Lawrence V. Fitz said, "Thank you for still offering opportunities for all of us to use our collective voices to contribute to something greater than our individual selves." Claire Manson contributed, "It was a joy to be a part of this Facebook group page, because I would receive daily notifications about inspirational quotes which would brighten up my day. Furthermore, digging up quotes myself and reflecting over them... encouraged me to share what I thought was important to remember throughout one's life." When asked, what inspired the quotes <u>they</u> shared, Fran Nielsen, Kurt's mother, replied, "They were inspired from my youth." Carl Nielsen, Kurt's father, replied, "They were the only clean ones I could think of." Kurt Nielsen, then summed up his family's responses by explaining, "Now you all understand where my humor came from!" According to Sabrina Ganier, "It's so nice being a part of this group and I was happy to contribute. Thank you for letting everyone in this group be a part of something so special." Vangie Obrero had this to say, "It has been an honor to contribute to a book filled with inspiration and spark. Thank you, Mr. Willert, for being the glue to bind our different perspectives together on these pages! It shows our interdependence on one another to keep us going and let us know... we are never alone." Anne Buccola Wiencek offered, "What a beautiful gift to be a part of a beautiful book that will bring joy and happiness to others through the years!" Linda Atherton explained, "When I was young, I was able to travel the world and beyond because of words skillfully crafted by writers who had something to share. Now, whether they be my own words or the words of others, I still tend to gravitate toward the thoughtful, ridiculous, kind, silly, meaningful, and life-affirming words that elicit strong emotions, and at the end of the day... I hold onto them like old friends... to be cherished and never forgotten." Finally, Jeanette Zapata shared, "It was wonderful and delightful to be able to contribute everything possible to this book filled with a whole lot of inspiration, love, positivity and uplifting sayings, all very valuable and great for others, all generations of the present and future to enjoy."

Thank you so much for supporting our efforts through picking up this book. I hope it brings you both joy and insight. '*Dave' Life Lines... Take Two*,' has been one of the most rewarding group projects I have ever been involved with! Putting this book together, as a team, was just as delightful as being a part of the team, itself! To be honest, I'm sorry to see this one-hundred-person strong, collaboration of friends and family end! We set out with this project, desiring to produce an inspiring and entertaining book for everyone, that would feature a broad array of different topics and viewpoints... and with everyone's help... I believe we've accomplished exactly that! Enjoy the ride!

Chapter One:
MOTIVATIONAL THOUGHTS!

There is a very broad collection of motivational thoughts and observations in this chapter, which cover everything from *not being lazy* to *creating perfection*! The main *gist* of it, however… is helping everyone to become more motivated to become happier and more successful in all parts of their lives. When you think about it, it's hard to achieve anything of lasting value without at least a little motivation, right? This chapter is dedicated to one of our contributing authors and a wonderful friend, *Marti Repp*. She is an inspiring person, and the hardest worker you will ever meet! She always makes time to help those in need… anyone… any time… and always with her happy and robust laugh and smile (her signature trademarks), that immediately fills the room with joy!

In her own words, she shares, *"I've always tried to follow "**The Golden Rule**," where you treat people the way that you want to be treated. There was a book written many years ago, called, '**Don't Sweat the Small Stuff**.' I took that to mean just relax and everything will turn out fine… the way it was meant to be. Another motivational thought I have always lived by, is, '**God grant me serenity to accept the things I cannot change, courage to change the things I can… and the wisdom to know the difference.'** My final motivational thoughts are to relax and enjoy your life, be kind to people and be smart. Life is precious and we are all human… and in this life together."*

Love to all,

Martha (Marti) Eileen Repp

"Enjoy every day, simple and true!"
(Marti Repp)

⸎⸎⸎

"It always takes a clear plan with a
distinct and strongly supported goal,
to give our all to a task... otherwise,
we're just spinning our wheels."

⸎⸎⸎

*"A true friendship is neither strengthened
by convenience or decree...
but by mutual desire."*

⌘⌘⌘⌘

*"Achieving success, always depends
on how badly we want it!"*

⌘⌘⌘⌘

*"As long as you live, don't waste a
moment, by being the person,
some OTHER people want you
to be... while forsaking your
true self in the process!"*

⌘⌘⌘⌘

*"The secret to staying motivated...
is to never be without a worthy goal!"*

⌘⌘⌘⌘

"The best way of finding something uniquely special... is to create it yourself."

❧❧❧

"Happiness can be very elusive... if you only work toward everyone else's!"

❧❧❧

"Nothing will kill a great employee faster... than watching <u>you</u> tolerate a bad one."
(Anon) (Shared by Lizabeth Guichard)

❧❧❧

"To achieve the marvelous, it is precisely the unthinkable... that must be thought!"
(Tom Robbins)
(Shared by Tassa Hampton-Varga)

❧❧❧

"The only thing better than singing...
is more singing!"
(Ella Fitzgerald)
(Shared by Lawrence Vondrake Fitz)

～⌒⌒⌒～

"We can purposely isolate ourselves
from others, thereby avoiding
messy relationships;
or we can deal with the messes...
and strive to live harmoniously."

～⌒⌒⌒～

"Being alive is miraculous! Let
every thought, word and deed we
produce... be worthy of it!"

～⌒⌒⌒～

"There is only one <u>foolproof</u> way to save money,
It's called... not spending all of it!"

～⌒⌒⌒～

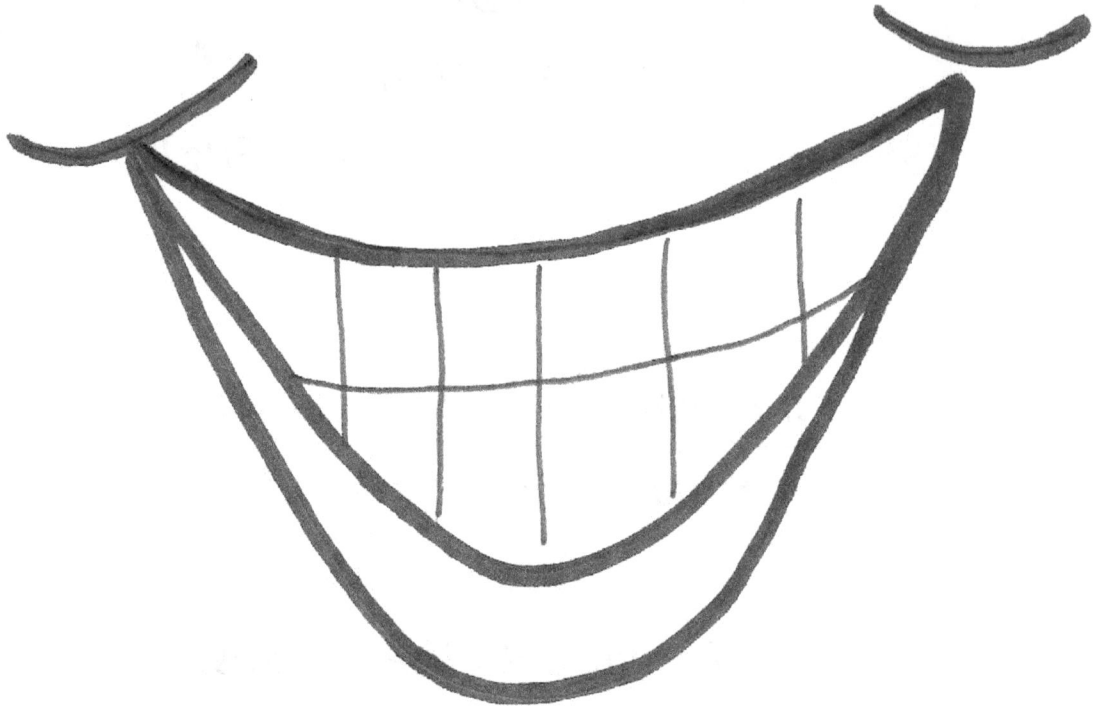

"Being told you're 'appreciated' is one of the simplest, yet most incredible things you can ever hear!" (Anon)

✒✒✒✒

"It's easy to criticize others, when <u>you've</u> never had the courage to do it yourself."
(Lori Halopoff-Fenelon)

✒✒✒✒

"The worth of something you have created,
is not found in other people's
assessments... but in your own heart."

⁓⁓⁓

"Tough times don't last...
tough people do!"
(Robert Schuler)
(Shared by Bill Kuhl)

⁓⁓⁓

"Courage is bravery in the face of fear...
with no assurance of a happy ending."

⁓⁓⁓

"Taking a positive journey of discovery,
is a vital and exciting part of everyone's
happiness... at any age."

⁓⁓⁓

"Don't take it personally, but always remember,
'Not everyone wants to play our games...
just because we do.'"

❦❦❦

"Life expectancy is so unpredictable.
There is absolutely no time to hate, to
put-off plans... or to be indecisive."

❦❦❦

"When two people have a problem, having it
solved by one of the people, to the exclusion
of the other... is a very bad idea."

❦❦❦

"In this world there is only ONE kind of person, who
always comes in a broad array of different talents,
desires, colors, genders and beliefs! Love everyone...
regardless of your differences."

❦❦❦

"To achieve something challenging, never begin... unless you fully intend to finish!"

❧❧❧

"Don't be afraid to be yourself, even if it means not being one of the cool kids."

❧❧❧

"It doesn't matter, one bit, if we don't receive any rewards for being kind and honest. Hopefully, rewards aren't our motivation!"

❧❧❧

"Don't expect the most out of life, if all you put into it... is the least!"

❧❧❧

"Don't dread your future... be grateful for it!"

❧❧❧

"Hope is the thing with feathers,
that perches in the soul,
and sings the tune, without the words,
and never stops... at all."
(Emily Dickinson)
(Shared by Jeanette Zapata)

⤬⤬⤬⤬⤬

"The Christmas season reminds us to
be kind, forgiving and thankful
for everything... including
the privilege of overeating!"

⤬⤬⤬⤬⤬

"Hold a grudge and part of you
is in chains from the anger.
Forgive, the chains fall off...
and you are instantly set free!"

⤬⤬⤬⤬⤬

"Anything worth having, is worth working for."

(Laura Ann Washington-Franklin)

တတတ

"Nobody ever wrote down a plan to be fat, lazy or stupid. Those things are what happen when you <u>don't</u> have a plan."

(Larry Winget)

တတတ

"A person can feel happy in any environment, rich or poor, healthy or sick... if they only focus their minds on the positive things!"

❧❧❧

"Don't allow the prospect of failure to stop you from pursuing your dreams. Sometimes just 'trying'... is enough."

❧❧❧

"A talented person may achieve a lot, to the best of their ability... but there is no end to the achievements of a talented and committed group!"

❧❧❧

"If you often feel differently around other people because you don't seem to have a lot in common... Embrace it! Be yourself! Be unique!"

❧❧❧

"You may not have conquered every challenge in your life... but as long as you're trying... anything is possible!"

❦❦❦

"A single act of kindness throws out roots in all directions, and the roots spring-up... and make trees."
(Amelia Earhart)
(Shared by Jeanette Zapata)

❦❦❦

"You can't calm the storm so stop trying. What you <u>can</u> do is calm yourself. The storm will pass."
(J. Hawkeye)
(Shared by Chrysti B. Lajoie)

❦❦❦

"Winning, does not always mean coming in first."

❦❦❦

"If the bad behavior of others has hurt you...
Rise, like the phoenix, from the ashes...
and proceed to have a wonderful life!"

∽∾∽∾∽∾

"Don't allow yourself to get sucked
into someone else's dream...
unless you feel just as
<u>passionately</u> about it
as they do!"

∽∾∽∾∽∾

"Never despair because not everyone
is thrilled about your great idea.
If you are excited by it...
then it deserves consideration!"

∽∾∽∾∽∾

"Common sense trumps rules, when the rules...
lack common sense!"

∽∾∽∾∽∾

"The mechanic that would perfect his work... must first sharpen his tools."
(Confucius)

❧❧❧

"When things don't immediately pan out, never lower your expectations, just raise your appreciation for what you have already accomplished... and keep on trying!"

❧❧❧

"On the other side of fear... lies freedom."
(Erin Garcia)

❧❧❧

"In life, do good things, make friends, and help others... but never forget to <u>have fun</u> while you're doing it!"

❧❧❧

"Be patient. Sometimes you have to go through the worst... to get the best!"
(Sabrina Ganier)

❧❧❧

"Don't seek attention... seek fulfillment."

❧❧❧

*"When it comes to choosing workaholism or
a work-life balance... I remind myself,
'your work doesn't love you back!'"*
(Yen Mai)

❧❧❧

*"One doesn't have to operate with
great malice to do great harm.
the absence of empathy and
understanding... are sufficient."*
(Charles M. Blow)

❧❧❧

*"Never underestimate another person's
potential... or their ultimate
ability to succeed!"*

❧❧❧

*"In creating, let everything be
your inspiration!"*

❧❧❧

"I will not die an unlived life.
I will not live in fear of falling
or catching fire...
I choose to risk my significance
so that which came to me as seed,
goes on as blossom,
and that which came to me as blossom...
goes out as fruit."
(Dawna Marcova)
(Shared by Tassa Hampton-Varga)

∽✺∽✺∽✺✺

"Having your whole heart in a project
does not guarantee that you'll succeed.
But even if you don't, it <u>does</u> guarantee
that you should have no regrets,
because you will always know...
that you gave it your very best!"

∽✺∽✺∽✺✺

"When you start seeing your worth...
you'll find it harder to stay around
people who don't!"
(Anon)

❧❧❧

"A lot of people ask, 'how?' The word, itself,
stands for, 'Hundreds Of Ways!'"
(Keree James)

❧❧❧

"Got the blues?
Put on a pair of tap shoes...
and tap your troubles away!"
(Kurt Nielsen)

❧❧❧

"We can always find the silver lining in
every situation, even if we have to
create it... ourselves!"

❧❧❧

"Hate and fear are the most frightening concepts known to man. Sometimes, they even control us! But in the long run, even <u>they,</u> cannot defeat the positive might of faith, hope and love!"

❧❧❧

"If you keep track of where you are going, and from where you have come... you will never lose your way!"

❧❧❧

"During tough times, remember, somehow, some way... everything will be okay!"
(Lori Halopoff-Fenelon)

❧❧❧

"If not you, then who?"
(Vangie Obrero)

❧❧❧

"Do everything with purpose!"

(Stan Knight)

***

"There's no <u>can't</u>... only try!" (Teresa Cimino)

***

"Yesterday is the past.

Tomorrow is the future.

But today is a gift.

That's why they call it... the present!"

(Anne Buccola-Wiencek)

❧❧❧

"Don't limit your challenges...

challenge your limits!"

(Anon)

(Shared by Marcia Holman)

❧❧❧

"Success is revealed in many ways.

Sometimes when we think we've failed,

in actuality, we have succeeded! We must

wait for the dust to settle to claim victory."

(Anon)

(Shared by Douglas Newton)

❧❧❧

"There is always much we want to learn,
but we can't hope to learn it all...
unless our <u>motivation</u>
matches our <u>desire</u>!"

⌘⌘⌘

"If what we believe comes expressly from the
heart... then we don't need agreement
from others to make it meaningful."

⌘⌘⌘

"Every morning when we wake up, our newest
adventure begins. Whether or not we look
forward to meeting it... will undoubtedly
affect our level of success!"

⌘⌘⌘

"If you have never attempted to do 'your best' at a
particular activity... then how do you know
you're as bad at it as you think you are?"

⌘⌘⌘

"Sometimes, thinking outside the box,
is merely considering, not only how
something may affect us... but how
it may affect everyone else, as well!"

✿✿✿

"Although no one can go back and
make a brand-new start, anyone
can start from now and make
a brand-new ending!"
(Carl Bard)
(Shared by Vangie Obrero)

✿✿✿

"No matter how good or bad you perceive your
life to be, wake up each morning... and
be thankful that you still have one!"
(Anon) (Shared by Marcia Holman)

✿✿✿

"There is much drudgery between first enthusiasm and achievement."

(Claire Manson)

*"Hard work beats talent when
talent doesn't work hard."*
(Anon) (Shared by Alex Willert)

❧❧❧

*"Those people who think their personal
beliefs are true and correct and therefore
should be mandatory for everyone...
don't really understand democracy!"*

❧❧❧

*"The easiest way to approach impending change
is to adapt, but if you really don't want to adapt...
then maybe you shouldn't change at all."*

❧❧❧

*"It does not matter how slowly you
go as long as you do not stop."*
(Confucius)

❧❧❧

*"Repeating words of wisdom and speaking
on behalf of the less fortunate, doesn't
necessarily make you a good person,
unless, as they say...
you truly practice what you preach!"*

ⵚⵚⵚ

*"All kids need a little help, a little hope
and someone who believes in them!"*
(Magic Johnson)
(Shared by Leonel Diaz)

ⵚⵚⵚ

*"Don't complain too much
about life's challenges.
Conquering them, often leads
you to becoming a stronger and
more understanding person!"*

ⵚⵚⵚ

"The man who asks a question, is a fool for a minute. The man who does <u>not</u> ask... is a fool for life."
(Confucius)

∽∾∽∾∽

"Those amongst us who are free spirits have little problem getting motivated... but we must be mindful of where our spontaneity... may ultimately lead us."

∽∾∽∾∽

"There's no straighter road to success than exceeding expectations... one day at a time."
(Robin Crow)
(Shared by Jeanette Zapata)

∽∾∽∾∽

"Anyone can share words of wisdom. But it takes sincerity from the giver, and belief from the taker... to bring them to life!"

∽∾∽∾∽

"Once we realize that everyone around us has their own set of dreams to accomplish, hopefully, we'll stop depending on them so much... and take charge of our own lives!"

⨯⨯⨯

"Convincing yourself that today is not right for working on an unpopular task... sounds very much like an excuse!"

⨯⨯⨯

"There is no way that there is 'no way'... Did you try?"
(Natalia Todorov)

⨯⨯⨯

"Be brave enough to 'suck' at something new!" (Anon)

⨯⨯⨯

"We become who we <u>need</u> to be, out of necessity.
But to become who we <u>want</u> to be... now
that takes some hard work, a little luck
and a whole lot of determination!"

❧❧❧❧

"Choose carefully. Unfortunately, some goals,
although they may seem attractive at first...
may prove to take more time, more effort
and more money than they are
ultimately worth!"

❧❧❧❧

"You never know how strong you are until
being strong...is the only choice you have!"
(Anon) (Shared by Mike Gash)

❧❧❧❧

"Even if you have the desire, achieving a challenging
goal often requires the determination and
motivation to <u>stick with it</u>... as long as it takes!"

❧❧❧❧

*"To accept and embrace someone exactly
as they are… is the purest form of love."*
(Erin Garcia)

⌘⌘⌘⌘⌘

"Being successful motivates us to do it again!"

⌘⌘⌘⌘⌘

*"The greatest freedom comes from
being fully and completely... who we are!"*
(Panache Desai)
(Shared by Jeanette Zapata)

❧❧❧❧

*"If you want to go far, don't slam
doors and burn bridges behind you...
because you will always end up
in the same place you started."*
(Natalia Todorov)

❧❧❧❧

*"Most of the time greatness comes from
ordinary people, who commit to something
with all of their hearts. Sadly, most people
sell themselves short, by never even
attempting it, for fear of failure.
Ironically, not trying... <u>is</u> failure."*

❧❧❧❧

"There are three ways to change the world...
with your words, with your deeds...
and with your prayers."
(Saint Faustina)
(Shared by Annie Accetta-Canet)

❧❧❧

"Don't let the past dictate the present.
Let go of what you thought life would be
and embrace where the journey has led you."
(Teresa Cimino)

❧❧❧

"The main reason we don't accomplish more
of the things we want to is because we
procrastinate and find more 'pressing'
things to take their place. When you
decide to attempt a worthy goal...
start it right then... and find
a way to finish it!"

❧❧❧

"Life is not about how you
survive the storm...
It's about how you dance
in the rain."
(Anon)

❧❧❧

"Being motivated isn't always easy
and can certainly be exhausting...
but man, does it help us to succeed!"

❧❧❧

"If you want a better life for yourself,
no matter how bad things are, avoid
endlessly complaining or relying too
heavily on others. Just go out there
armed with determination... and
build it yourself... using your
dreams as your guide."

❧❧❧

*"You will never reach your destination
if you stop and throw stones at
every dog that barks."*
(Sir Winston Churchill)
(Shared by Natalia Todorov)

*"It doesn't matter how messed-up the
world is around you. A positive
person can always deal with that...
by building happiness from within."*

*"To be successful, financially and/or artistically,
is a wonderful thing. But if you have
the love of family and friends...
you are TRULY BLESSED!"*
(Gene Nobles)

*"Good actions give strength to ourselves
and inspire good actions in others."*
(Plato)
(Shared by Jeanette Zapata)

⚬⚬⚬

*"Feeling like the best at something,
is not nearly as fulfilling as helping
someone else improve from feeling like
they are the worst... at the very same thing."*

⚬⚬⚬

*"Nothing astonishes men so much as
plain dealing and common sense."*
(Ralph Waldo Emerson)
(Shared by Douglas Newton)

⚬⚬⚬

*"Working toward an exciting and
worthy goal... is always in style."*

⚬⚬⚬

"Watch a spider rebuild, immediately after its web has been knocked down. Such a 'perfect' role model!"

"Sometimes music is the only
medicine the heart and soul need."
(Anon)
(Shared by Douglas Newton)

∽✺∽✺∽

"A negative mind will never
give you a positive life."
(Anon)
(Shared by Vincent Washington)

∽✺∽✺∽

"If we spent more time <u>doing</u> the things
we wanted to do and less time
just <u>talking</u> about them...
we would surely become achievers!"

∽✺∽✺∽

"A lack of motivation <u>never</u> makes
a goal any less worthy."

∽✺∽✺∽

"Never worry about who will be offended if you speak the truth. Worry about who will be misled, deceived and destroyed if you don't."
(Anon)
(Shared by Chrissie Casey-Brockman)

❧❧❧

"The greatest discovery of my generation, is that a human being can change his life by changing his attitude."
(William James)
(Shared by Chris Breyer)

❧❧❧

"Love strong, worry less, laugh often, dream big, sparkle more and shine bright!"
(Tassa Hampton-Varga)

❧❧❧

"A person who feels appreciated...
will always do more than is expected."
(Anon)

❧❧❧

"Being rich does not make you happy,
any more than being poor.
Being happy is not based on economics...
it's based on love."

❧❧❧

"Your life offers you a wonderful opportunity
to experience it in any way you choose!
But just like playing a game, it's much
more fun when others, of like minds
and hearts... are playing too!"

❧❧❧

"A goal without determination... is D.O.A."

❧❧❧

*"Beware. Feeling too self-important,
often leads to believing you have
an excuse for acting rudely."*

⚬⚬⚬⚬

*"No matter how you feel:
Get Up, Dress Up, Show Up
and never Give Up!"*
(Anon) (Shared by Douglas Newton)

⚬⚬⚬⚬

*"If you see someone without a smile...
give them one of yours."*
(Dolly Parton)
(Shared by Jeanette Zapata)

⚬⚬⚬⚬

*"Believing that every personal crisis is
something you will ultimately overcome...
is precisely the reason you will!"*

⚬⚬⚬⚬

*"Courage is the first of human qualities
because it is the quality that
guarantees all others."*
(Sir Winston Churchill)

⚬⚬⚬

*"The difference between a successful person
and others, is not a lack of strength,
not a lack of knowledge...
but rather a lack of will."*
(Vince Lombardi)

⚬⚬⚬

*"Everybody needs beauty as well as bread,
places to play in and places to pray in,
where nature may heal and give
strength to body and soul."*
(John Muir)
(Shared by Jeanette Zapata)

⚬⚬⚬

*"If you want something you've never had,
then you've got to do something
you've never done."*

(Anon) (Shared by Sarah Turner)

"Imagination rules the world!"
(Napoleon Bonaparte)
(Shared by Catherine Foley)

❧❧❧

"Fear never seems to get better by itself.
It's a terrible condition that strips us of
our self-worth, confidence and courage.
There is only one remedy... to meet
the fear head-on and vanquish it!"

❧❧❧

"When times get tough, relax and take
some deep breaths... and remember,
there's always tomorrow!"
(Marti Repp)

❧❧❧

"We don't 'find' our home... we 'create' it!"

❧❧❧

"Kind hearts are the gardens,
Kind words are the roots,
Kind thoughts are the flowers,
Kind deeds are the fruits.
Take care of your garden,
And keep out the weeds,
Fill it with sunshine...
Kind words and kind deeds."
(H.W. Longfellow)
(Shared by Jeanette Zapata)

❦❦❦

"Taking something seriously...
guarantees we will give it our
best effort. Shouldn't that
define everything we do?"

❦❦❦

"Don't dream of winning... Train for it!"
(Mo Farrah) (Shared by Chrysti B. Lajoie)

❦❦❦

"It's not 'what' we have in life, but WHO,
we have in our lives that matters most."
(Anon) (Shared by Douglas Newton)

❧❦❧

"Where there's hope, there's life.
It fills us with fresh courage...
and makes us strong again."
(Anne Frank) (Shared by Jeanette Zapata)

❧❦❧

"Don't forget that you are made of three
different parts – body, mind and
soul. Do something nice
for each part every day!"
(Natalia Todorov)

❧❦❧

"Sweetness or kindness in any form...
always makes me smile."

❧❦❧

*"Any time I am happily laughing...
it's never a wasted day!"*

༄ઝ৫৲

*"A simple rule to live by, nicknamed
'the baby philosophy' is...
'If it stinks... change it!'"
(Anon)*

༄ઝ৫৲

*"If we fill our lives with the hopes and
dreams of our hearts as well as the
love and friendship of others...
what more could we ask for?"*

༄ઝ৫৲

*"Courage is not letting your actions
be influenced by your fears."
(Arthur Koestler)
(Shared by Chrysti B. Lajoie)*

༄ઝ৫৲

"Achievements, regardless of how small or insignificant they may seem... should always be worn as internal badges of pride and satisfaction."

⁂

"Dreaming of better days won't necessarily make them come any sooner, but it won't keep them away, either. And most importantly... it will sure feel better while we are waiting!"

⁂

"Once you've been to hell and back... there's not much left to fear." (Anon)

⁂

"Wanna get your wheels going? Replace SOMEDAY with TODAY!" (Natalia Todorov)

⁂

"I have nothing in common with lazy people
who blame others for their lack of success.
Great things come from hard work
and perseverance. No excuses!"
(Kobe Bryant) (Shared by Vangie Obrero)

"Although bullying or threatening behavior may turn you a quick profit, remember, in the long run, we reap what we sow... and I fear if you sow that kind of behavior, you will eventually find yourself <u>short</u> on friends, a bright future... and happiness!"

❧❧❧❧

"The truth of the matter is that achieving something without joy... sucks!"

❧❧❧❧

"As soon as I open my eyes, each morning... I just know it will be a good day!"

❧❧❧❧

"Character is doing the right thing... when nobody's looking."
(J.C. Watts)

❧❧❧❧

"A pessimist sees the difficulty in every opportunity; an optimist sees the <u>opportunity</u> in every difficulty."

(Sir Winston Churchill)

(Shared by Natalia Todorov)

❦❦❦

"I'll never quit trying to improve myself, because I believe life is about reinventing who we are... until we get it right!"

❦❦❦

"Knowing is not enough, we must <u>apply</u>! Willing is not enough... we must <u>do</u>!"

(Bruce Lee) (Shared by Shun L. Griffin)

❦❦❦

"Even when I get scared... I still saddle up!"

(John Wayne) (Shared by James Willert)

❦❦❦

"After experiencing a debilitating accident or illness, be sure <u>not</u> to put all of your trust exclusively in the professionals. Taking personal charge of our own effort and motivation... will work wonders!"

∽∾∽∾∽∾

"Through adversity, the struggle... always leads us to the answer." (Doug Kuhl)

∽∾∽∾∽∾

"For every set-back we experience, there is a potential success story out there... just waiting for us to embrace!"

∽∾∽∾∽∾

"Life is like a professional boxing match. In order to have a chance to succeed, you've got to get up... each time you are knocked down!"

∽∾∽∾∽∾

*"When we stop categorizing people by
things like color, age, wealth, religion,
beauty or social standing...
we begin to see each individual,
regardless of those things,
for who they really are.
Everyone deserves to be known that way."*

❧❧❧

*"Shoot for the moon and even if you
miss... you'll be among the stars."*
(Anon)
(Shared by Tassa Hampton-Varga)

❧❧❧

*"Something only matters to you...
if you <u>make it</u> matter.
Everything is not dust in the wind...
unless you relegate it so."*

❧❧❧

"In order to seek the truth, without bias, one must be open to the possibility that it may turn out to be 'different,'... from what we had expected."

⤙⤙⤙

"I've learned that it's important in life... to always have a 'Plan B!'"

⤙⤙⤙

"Good morning world! Smile, stay positive, and give your best to yourself and those around you. Miracles happen every day!"
(Wendy Miguel)

⤙⤙⤙

"When life gives you scraps... make quilts!"
(Frances Nielsen)
(Shared by Kurt Nielsen)

⤙⤙⤙

Chapter Two:
POSITIVE THOUGHTS!

It's hard to imagine *positive thoughts* apart from *positive achievements,* and that's because one naturally… follows the other. In addition to being motivated, positive thinking is a mandatory component of achievement through providing *patience*, otherwise you would be likely to quit working on a project after experiencing that first setback. This Chapter is dedicated to *Bill Kuhl,* a contributing author and a wonderful family friend who has kept everyone around him smiling, for decades! He is also one of the most positive people I have ever known! He deals with life like he deals with people… through his quick wit and his kind heart. Bill perfectly exemplifies the '*positiveness,*' found throughout this chapter.

As he so eloquently states, *"It's easy to be negative, especially when things aren't going your way. It takes commitment, determination and a whole lotta guts to be optimistic in the face of adversity. No matter what your circumstances, the world will go on and you will, too. So why not move forward with a smile and a positive attitude? You'll find that positivity is infectious; not only do you make others feel good, but the satisfaction of helping others will fuel your motivation to continue spreading joy. The late, Kobe Bryant said,* **'Life is too short to get bogged down and be discouraged. You have to keep moving.'** *So, chin up, stay positive, and get going!"*

Sincerely,

Bill Kuhl

"How you do everything...
is how you do anything!"
(Martha Beck) (Shared by Bill Kuhl)

"Respect everyone's right to express their own opinions... and hopefully they will respect your right to disagree."

✨✨✨

"Never allow your busy life to prohibit you from doing those things that are <u>most</u> important to you."

✨✨✨

"I was born to make mistakes... not to fake perfection!"
(Amo Mama)
(Shared by Natalia Todorov)

✨✨✨

"Be inspired when you do artistic things, not only for fame and fortune... but to quench that ferocious thirst inside of you."

✨✨✨

"Think happy, do happy... be happy!"

❦❦❦❦

*"Happiness is not gained by what we have
and what we know... but by what
we <u>do</u> with them."*

❦❦❦❦

*"Regardless of the severity of our troubles,
we should always focus on our blessings
and strengths... and have faith that
somehow, they will guide us to
resolving our problems."*

❦❦❦❦

*"We will never forget those things we believe
we would like to achieve in our lives...
even when we can't seem to find
the motivation to pursue them."*

❦❦❦❦

*"When you feel down, simply adopting
a positive attitude is promising
yourself that things will somehow,
get better... and they usually do!"*

⌒⌒⌒

*"For every minute you are angry...
you lose sixty seconds of happiness."*
(Ralph Waldo Emerson)
(Shared by Chrysti B. Lajoie)

⌒⌒⌒

*"Patience is one of the greatest
virtues of life."*
(Bill Repp) (Shared by Marti Repp)

⌒⌒⌒

*"Although our lives continue to change
every day, the one constant is the love we
feel for others... and they for us."*

⌒⌒⌒

"Taking your own advice is always prudent, because that's the best way to find out... if it's any good!"

❦❦❦

"Good solutions, are a direct result of thinking positively!"

❦❦❦

"Some days are not innately happy and may need a little help!"

❦❦❦

"The future belongs to those who believe in the beauty of their dreams."
(Eleanor Roosevelt)
(Shared by Marcia Holman)

❦❦❦

"One, is not a lot... but it's a positive start!"

❦❦❦

"When people laugh at your thoughts, just remember,
'One person's trash is another one's treasure.'
Don't ever let anyone stop your creative
mind from doing its thing!"

⁓⧏⧏⧏⁓

"Anyone can find a possible 'solution'
for any problem, with the only
downside being, that they may
not arrive at the 'best solution,'
on their first attempt...
It's called, 'creative brainstorming!'"

⁓⧏⧏⧏⁓

"The best way to handle tough times is
to find and nurture the positive...
There is always a positive!"

⁓⧏⧏⧏⁓

"Beauty is an integral part of everything!"

⁓⧏⧏⧏⁓

"A set-back is just a set-up...
for something better."
(Romeo Rodriguez)
(Shared by Lawrence Vondrake Fitz)

⚬⚬⚬⚬⚬

"I believe there are plenty of people in the
world who are kind, honest and
compassionate. They are the ones
who keep making the world
a better place...
by serving as our role models!"

⚬⚬⚬⚬⚬

"Never make, 'agreeing on everything,'
a prerequisite for friendship.
The disagreements you may have
between you, could very well
be fertile ground...
for mutual growth and respect."

⚬⚬⚬⚬⚬

"Savor the journey." (Tassa Hampton-Varga)

"Don't ever take a good friendship for granted.
Like everything else of value in life...
it really benefits from your regular attention."

⸎⸎⸎⸎

"If you don't know what you really want out of life...
then now is as good a time as any to
start thinking about it!"

⸎⸎⸎⸎

"A road called 'Later' will lead
you to a place called 'Never.'"
(Natalia Todorov)

⸎⸎⸎⸎

"The ones who travel the road of life with you,
day in and day out, are often best suited to
speak into your attitudes and behaviors."
(Bobby Schuler)
(Shared by Douglas Newton)

⸎⸎⸎⸎

"People don't plan to fail... they fail to plan."

(Lori Halopoff-Fenelon)

⌘⌘⌘

"The best time to make a decision is when we're free of guilt, threat, anger, depression, fear and addiction. Only then, do we honestly know... what it is we really want!"

⌘⌘⌘

"You can learn a lot about a person by observing how they handle adversity."

⌘⌘⌘

"If you spend your life making your small corner of the world a little safer, a little kinder and a little happier for you and those around you... then you have done well!"

⌘⌘⌘

"When you have an important life goal you want to reach... as long as you live, you never have to set a deadline!"

∽∽∽∽

"Although the world tries to tempt you with other things... there is really nothing comparable to sincere love and friendship!"

∽∽∽∽

"If you suffer from anxiety, don't allow it to spoil your day. Your concerns will eventually work themselves out, one way or another... whether you worry about them or not!"

∽∽∽∽

"I can show you better... than I can tell you."
(Lawrence Vondrake Fitz)

∽∽∽∽

"A child is going to remember who was there, not what you spent on them. Kids outgrow a toy and outfits... but they never outgrow time and love."

(Anon) (Shared by Yolanda Setoodeh)

"Stress is simply the belief that everything is an emergency." (Amanda Moh)

∽∽∽∽

"He who falls in love with himself... has no rivals."
(Benjamin Franklin)
(Shared by Yolanda Rodriguez)

∽∽∽∽

"One of the most exciting parts of our realities... is when we witness our deepest dreams becoming real!"

∽∽∽∽

"As they say, 'Age is just a number.' If you enjoy your life, avoid worry and act wisely... you will always have better things to do than to fret about your age!"

∽∽∽∽

"The Lord is close to those
whose hearts are broken."
(Psalm 34:18a)
(Shared by Cheri Hale-Patterson)

⁂

"They say time changes things...
but you actually have to
<u>change them</u> yourself!"
(Andy Warhol)
(Shared by Drea Silva)

⁂

"When you get upset, you give yourself
two jobs... getting upset and trying
to make yourself happy again.
I prefer to have only one job."
(Betty Gardea)

⁂

"You cannot do a kindness too soon,
for you never know how soon...
it will be too late."
(Ralph Waldo Emerson)
(Shared by Jeanette Zapata)

⚬⚬⚬

"Trying to please everyone is an impossibility,
no matter how hard you try. Since you'll be
spending your entire life with yourself...
why not start there?"

⚬⚬⚬

"A person should not forget two
important lessons –
to use things, not people;
and to love people, not things."
(Anon) (Shared by Natalia Todorov)

⚬⚬⚬

"Comparing your skills to others is a detriment to growth. Don't waste your energy just trying to beat great competitors... be <u>inspired</u> by them to grow and to improve."

ɷɷɷ

"If it ain't broke, don't fix it!"
(Amy Wells)

ɷɷɷ

"It's never too late to start over, as long as your new plan is potentially better... than your last one!"

ɷɷɷ

"The way you look on the outside may seem important to you... but it's what you have in your heart... that matters the most."
(Marti Repp)

ɷɷɷ

"When you love and feel loved,
everything you do somehow...
becomes more meaningful!"

❧

"Patience is the calm acceptance that
things can happen in a different order
than the one you have in mind."
(David Allen)
(Shared by Jeanette Zapata)

❧

"There are many good reasons to
tell the truth, be kind and to love.
There are also many reasons not to...
but none of them are any good."

❧

"It's no shame to stray from the crowd."

❧

*"Be so positive that negative people
don't want to be around you!"
(Anon) (Shared by Tami Seaton)*

❧❧❧

*"The two most important tools I learned
in my youth were, 'to think for myself'
and to always reserve the right, 'to disagree.'
They don't necessarily make my life any easier...
but I always feel better about my decisions!"*

❧❧❧

*"Trust doesn't come with a refill. Once it's gone, you
probably won't get it back, and if you do...
it will never be the same!" (By Tab D'Biassi)
(Shared by Laura Ann Washington-Franklin)*

❧❧❧

"In the end, <u>love</u>, is still the most precious thing!"

❧❧❧

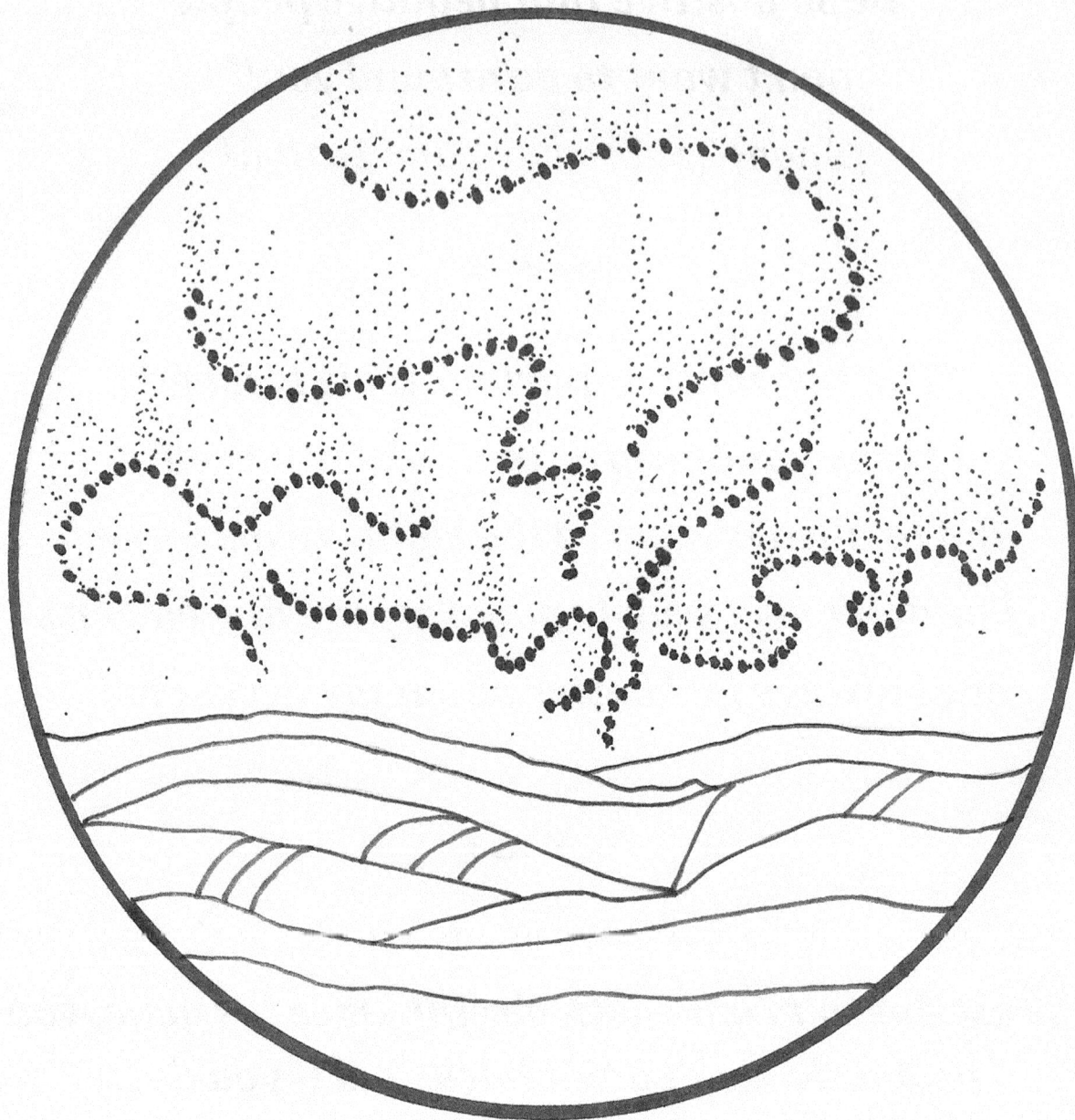

"Always be on the lookout for the presence of wonder."
(Ruth Ellis)

"Education is what survives when what has been learned has been long forgotten."
(BF Skinner)

❧❧❧

"Your value doesn't decrease based on someone's inability to see your worth."
(Anon)
(Shared by Stephanie Miller)

❧❧❧

"Worrying won't stop the bad stuff from happening... It just stops you from enjoying the good!"
(Anon)

❧❧❧

"There is such beauty... such bravery... in starting anew, each and every day."
(S.C. Lourie)
(Shared by Jeanette Zapata)

❧❧❧

"Everyone has friendships. The trouble is, they become dormant whenever we are busy. But don't fret. A simple phone call ought to bring them right back to life!"

❦❦❦

"Don't let yesterday take up too much of today."

(Anon)

❦❦❦

"When gratitude becomes your default setting... life changes."

(Nancy Leigh DeMoss)

(Shared by Jeanette Zapata)

❦❦❦

"Living each moment like it's special, is a great reminder... that it is!"

❦❦❦

"Don't believe everything you hear. If the world was really as bad as some people paint it... we would already be gone! Save yourself some worrying. Always figure things out for yourself!"

❧❧❧

"Courage doesn't always ROAR! Sometimes courage is the quiet voice at the end of the day, saying, 'I will try again tomorrow!'"
(Mary Anne Radmacher)
(Shared by Marcia Holman)

❧❧❧

"We're born, we live and we die. Make the 'living part' meaningful every day of your life."

❧❧❧

"It is up to you to see the beauty of everyday things." (Jeanette Zapata)

❧❧❧

"Earning a decent living and meeting your responsibilities is very important...

But it's what you <u>do</u> with the

'rest' of your life...

that really defines you!"

◈◈◈◈◈

"Personal opinions can be a great divider of people. Share at your own risk!"

◈◈◈◈◈

"More is learned from hardship than comfort.

Real wisdom is refined in

crucible of affliction."

(Chrissie Casey-Brockman)

◈◈◈◈◈

"There's no such thing as a wasted day...

only a misguided one!"

◈◈◈◈◈

"I believe kindness is a wonderful and magical thing. It does not cost anything to be kind. How beautiful, right?" *(Samantha Dizon)*

ᑲᑲᑲᑲᑲ

"Treat everyone you meet, as a friend."

ᑲᑲᑲᑲᑲ

"A negative attitude is to a person...
what a lack of wings would
be to an eagle."

❧❧❧

"Get to the point. Just open your mouth and tell
people what you need, want or expect!"
(Lawrence Vondrake Fitz)

❧❧❧

"One of the most wonderful double blessings a
person can possess, is one, to be unafraid
to <u>ask</u> for help whenever needed...
and two... to <u>give</u> help freely,
whenever the situation is reversed."

❧❧❧

"Don't get sucked into another person's rage.
You'll end up feeling angry, but curiously...
you probably won't really understand why."

❧❧❧

"It is so easy to dwell on what is wrong in our lives... but it is much more beneficial, if we simply appreciate... all that is right!"

⋙⋘

"The simplest lessons in life, are generally, the most meaningful. Everything else... just sort of makes our lives more interesting."

⋙⋘

"Be careful of who you trust. Salt and sugar look the same!" (Anon) (Shared by Tami Seaton)

⋙⋘

"If talking about a certain person makes you angry... maybe you should <u>stop</u> talking about them?"

⋙⋘

"If no one else will help you...
do it yourself!"
(Stan Knight)

❧❧❧❧

"There can be quite a difference between 'doing the right thing,' and merely 'pleasing someone.' Be sure you are doing things for the right reasons."

❧❧❧❧

"Being a positive person does not require you to always have to rattle off positive phrases. It's far more important that your heart remains forever hopeful!"

❧❧❧❧

"Be generous with your smile!"
(Lori Halopoff-Fenelon)

❧❧❧❧

"Happiness is spending time with kind and positive people."

✆✆✆

"Don't wait for things to get better. Life will always be complicated. Learn to be happy right now!"
(Natalia Todorov)

✆✆✆

"Believing in yourself is the first rule of feeling confident... and the second and the third!"

✆✆✆

"Never dwell on the past. Just live and learn, while putting one foot in front of the other."
(Barbara Kovacs-Minar)

✆✆✆

*"Creating an uncomplicated life of simple
pleasures and minor problems...
begins with our choices."*

⸎⸎⸎

*"A beautiful face will age and a perfect body
will change, but a beautiful soul
will always remain... a beautiful soul."*
(Anon)
(Shared by Linda Atherton)

⸎⸎⸎

*"When you speak or write, know that
although your choice of words
may be beautiful,
too many of them...
may obscure your message."*

⸎⸎⸎

"The best thing about going to sleep... is waking up."

⸎⸎⸎

"As good as it was to play as a child... it does not compare to watching your own kids play!"

(Jerry Halpin)

⊱⊰⊱⊰⊱

"You'll never know your favorite flavor of ice cream... until you try them all!"

(Kurt Nielsen)

⊱⊰⊱⊰⊱

"Be teachable. We are
not always right!"
(Tassa Hampton-Varga)

❧❧❧

"Regrets from the past are always meant
to be supplanted by hope for the
present and future!"

❧❧❧

"Always know the difference between
taking something seriously...
or taking it personally!"

❧❧❧

"Honesty may not always be the easiest
thing to do in difficult situations,
but nevertheless...
it's always the best policy!"
(Influenced by Benjamin Franklin)

❧❧❧

"Don't ever give up! A humble beginning combined with a positive attitude and determination... should eventually lead anyone to success!"

～～～

"Do at least one thing each day... that will make you happy!"
(Anon)

～～～

"We are not truly free, until we are willing to think and express for ourselves!"

～～～

"Creativity is the magical tool... that saves us all from boredom!"

～～～

"Never apologize for having high standards.
People who really want to be in your
life, will rise up to meet them."
(Ziad Adelinour)
(Shared by Tassa Hampton-Varga)

❧❦❧

"Just because the majority of people believe
something is true, doesn't mean that it is.
Remember when almost everyone
believed the Earth was flat?"

❧❦❧

"Nothing fixes a misunderstanding better
than the giving and receiving of a
sincere... 'I'm sorry.'"

❧❦❧

"One, 'yes,' is better than a thousand, 'maybe's!'"

❧❦❧

"Perfection can be very subjective, so it's unfair to hold anyone, including yourself, to its high, and everchanging standards. Just strive to always do your best and then some... while simultaneously encouraging everyone else to do the same thing!"

⚬⚬⚬⚬

"You know you have a positive attitude when although everything went wrong today, you can't wait until tomorrow... to make it right!"

⚬⚬⚬⚬

"Apologizing does not always mean you're wrong and the other person is right. It just means you value your relationship... more than your ego." (Anon)

⚬⚬⚬⚬

"Give a smile to a stranger. It might be the only sunshine they see all day!" (Keree James)

*"To make a difference in someone's life,
you do not have to be brilliant,
rich, beautiful or perfect...
You just have to care."*
(Mandy Hale)
(Shared by Jeanette Zapata)

❧❧❧

*"To avoid the pitfalls of life,
stay one step ahead of what WILL
eventually happen... and two steps
ahead of what COULD!"*

❧❧❧

*"Remember, being happy doesn't mean
you have it all. It simply means you're
thankful for all you have."* *(Anon)*
(Shared by Linda Atherton)

❧❧❧

"Excessive pride and narcissism may lead to alienating the people around you. But simply <u>feeling proud</u> of your achievements... now, that's what success is all about!"

⸎⸎⸎

"If we approach every new truth without bias or preconceived interpretation and with an open mind... we have a far greater chance of understanding it!"
(Inspired by Vangie Obrero)

⸎⸎⸎

"Never equate your self-worth by your number of friends, personal accolades or the amount of money you have. Base it on whether or not you are living your life... the way that you want to!"

⸎⸎⸎

"Dispensing with the guilt and anger and replacing them with hopeful thoughts... is the first step toward building a positive attitude for yourself."

∽∾∽∾∽∾

"When given the choice between being right and being kind... choose kind."
(R.J. Palacio)
(Shared by Samantha Dizon)

∽∾∽∾∽∾

"I read that thinking positively and being hopeful, helps fight off illness and may even lead to a longer life! Imagine that?"

∽∾∽∾∽∾

"Extra time may be a blessing or a curse,
depending on how we use it.
Remember the wise, old saying,
'Life is meant to be lived?'
Well... do it!"

∽∂∽∂∽∂

"It's okay for you to believe what you believe...
It's not okay for you to demand others
believe the same way."
(Anon)
(Shared by Linda Atherton)

∽∂∽∂∽∂

"When you are a positive thinker,
you can find something hopeful
in just about any situation...
even when others don't
immediately see it!"

∽∂∽∂∽∂

"Tearing down others and yelling out how bad they are... does nothing to convince anyone else of how good 'you' are."

❧

"When things get tough, expect them to improve with all your heart... Faith can move mountains."

❧

"Be patient. Positive thinking and experience tell us that everything always gets better with time."

❧

"The darkest nights produce the brightest stars."
(Wendy Miguel)

❧

"Loving yourself is not a bad thing...
as long as you love everyone else too."

∽∾∽∾∽∾

"Each person resides in two worlds; the outside
and the inside. When the outside becomes
limited by circumstances beyond our control,
we can readily turn to the inside...
which is as limitless as we allow it to be."
(Natalia Todorov)

∽∾∽∾∽∾

"Don't hate those who may seem arrogant
and unconcerned about anyone else. Feel
sorry for them and if they are in need
someday... be the first to help them."
(Inspired by Charles Dickins'
story, 'A Christmas Carol.')

∽∾∽∾∽∾

"No matter how invested you are in your beliefs, always remain open minded, enabling you to alter them... if you are so moved."

❧❧❧❧

"In life, there is <u>never</u> only one right answer."

❧❧❧❧

"For every set-back we experience, there is a potential 'success story'... just waiting for us to embrace."

❧❧❧❧

"Every decision we make, leads to an action, which eventually, creates a key for us to open the door to the consequences; good, bad or indifferent. Don't be afraid of making some wrong decisions, because usually, that's just part of life. But, be sure to <u>learn</u> from them!"

❧❧❧❧

"Try to be a rainbow in someone else's cloud!"
(Amaya Angelou)
(Shared by Marcia Holman)

❦❦❦

"Being tenaciously inquisitive,
always leads to questions,
which in time... will lead to answers!"

❦❦❦

"Just as soon as you decide the
excitement in your life is gone...
it's about time to start a new adventure!"

❦❦❦

"Trust in the gifts that God has given you!"

❦❦❦

"Hope springs eternal." *(Alexander Pope)*

❦❦❦

"Love everybody, no matter what.

Even if people are icky... try love instead!"

(Ruth Jane Willert)

*"Always make time to do those things
you enjoy, even though you may be
busy with the mundane side of life.
'Happiness' always trumps
'busy' in our memories."*

⮦⮦⮦

*"Good parenting is teaching your kids
how to be responsible and independent,
know right from wrong, and also
how to love and respect. Then...
give them the freedom to fly!"*
(Natalia Todorov)

⮦⮦⮦

*"Imagine the greatness this world would
know if kindness were as contagious
as the common cold."*
(Richelle E. Goodrich)
(Shared by Jeanette Zapata)

⮦⮦⮦

"Sometimes common sense...

isn't all that common."

(Lori Halopoff-Fenelon)

❧❧❧

"At the touch of love...

everyone becomes a poet."

(Plato)

(Shared by Jeanette Zapata)

❧❧❧

"Nobody's perfect, but that doesn't mean

we should ever stop trying to be!"

❧❧❧

"Not procrastinating,

is not so much about finding

the time to do something...

as it is <u>being motivated</u> to do it."

❧❧❧

"Rejection is God's protection."
(Pamela Cummins)
(Shared by Colleen Caron)

∽☙∽☙∽

"Being life-long friends does not require
seeing or even talking to each other frequently.
It does, however, require love and knowledge
that each time you do see each other...
it will feel as if no time has passed."
(Teresa Cimino)

∽☙∽☙∽

"A positive attitude does not rid your
world of worry... but it does provide
hope and strength for overcoming
any negative situation."

∽☙∽☙∽

"Sustained faith makes <u>anything</u> possible."

∽☙∽☙∽

"Enjoy life today, because yesterday is gone and tomorrow is never promised."

(Anon)

(Shared by Sabrina Ganier)

≪≪≫≫

"Each day comes bearing its own gifts."

(Ruth Ann Schabacker)

(Shared by Jeanette Zapata)

≪≪≫≫

"Never judge your friends. If you mutually feel better having each other around… then just appreciate that!"

≪≪≫≫

"You can't get so hung up on who you'd rather be that you forget to make the most of who you are now." *(Anon)*

(Shared by Lizabeth Guichard)

≪≪≫≫

"Life is a series of thousands of
tiny miracles. Notice them."
(Anon)

⌘⌘⌘

"A smart man knows what to say…
A wise man knows whether or not to say it!"
(Gene Nobles)

⌘⌘⌘

"Time will pass and the years will fly by…
so why not spend that time
pursuing your dreams?"
(Lori Halopoff-Fenelon)

⌘⌘⌘

"Never go to bed with dirty
dishes in the sink."
(Frances Nielsen)
(Shared by Kurt Nielsen)

⌘⌘⌘

"Ego is overdressed insecurity."

(Quincy Jones)

(Shared by Vangie Obrero)

⌘⌘⌘

"To stay positive, think about, watch, read,

say and listen to as many uplifting

things as you possibly can!

And do the same thing tomorrow…

and the next day… and forever!"

⌘⌘⌘

"Make good choices."

(Lizsa & Kevin Pinedo)

⌘⌘⌘

"The 'why' is always more important…

than the 'what'."

(Lawrence Vondrake Fitz)

⌘⌘⌘

Family
Friends
Health
Happiness
Faith

"In a society that has you counting money, pounds, calories and steps, be a rebel... and count your blessings instead."

(Lisa Heckman) (Shared by Rita Jones)

"Facts do not cease to exist just because they are ignored."
(Aldous Huxley)
(Shared by Chrysti B. Lajoie)

∽∾∽∾∽

"Negativity is like a dead fish...
it stinks up the place after a while."
(Betty Gardea)

∽∾∽∾∽

"Hustle in silence and let your success make the noise!"
(Anon)
(Shared by Laura Ann Washington-Franklin)

∽∾∽∾∽

"We only die once... but we live every day!"
(Anon)
(Shared by Greg Wells)

∽∾∽∾∽

"Hope thrives within a positive attitude."

❦❦❦

"Music is a more potent instrument than any other for education because rhythm and harmony find their way into the inward places of the soul."
(Plato)   (Shared by Douglas Newton)

❦❦❦

"We don't know what the future holds… but we do know 'who' holds the future."
(Leticia Garcia)

❦❦❦

"In times of crisis, we finally act like humans, and are strong together… <u>for</u> each other!"
(Kathy Walborn)

❦❦❦

"Know the value of time; snatch, seize, and enjoy every moment of it."
(Lord Chesterfield)
(Shared by Jeanette Zapata)

❧❧❧

"Walk slowly, breathe deeply, do selfless deeds... and enjoy mother nature."
(Natalia Todorov)

❧❧❧

"Just because someone claims to hate you... doesn't mean that you have to reciprocate."

❧❧❧

"All of us are better when we are loved."
(Alistair Macleod)
(Shared by Douglas Newton)

❧❧❧

109

"Live your life as you feel you were born to.
No apologies necessary!"

⚬⚬⚬⚬⚬

"When a stranger says something to
you that unintentionally insults you,
don't take offense, or it may also...
'unintentionally' hurt your feelings."

⚬⚬⚬⚬⚬

"If you can't do anything about it,
then let it go. Don't be a prisoner
to things you can't change."
(Tony Gaskins)
(Shared by Marylen Ayash-Borgen)

⚬⚬⚬⚬⚬

"I wonder why it is, that just <u>thinking</u> about
a happy thought... makes us smile?"

⚬⚬⚬⚬⚬

*"We don't build the lives we want by
saving time... we build the lives
we want and then time saves itself."*
(Laura Vanderkam)
(Shared by Natalia Todorov)

⤜⤚⤜⤚

*"Don't ever take a fence down, until you
know the reason why it was put up."*
(G.K. Chesterton)
(Shared by Linda Atherton)

⤜⤚⤜⤚

*"It is always important, especially during times
like these, to look at the positive in every day.
Good days or bad, there is always something
within the day that can make you smile...
if you look closely enough."*
(Samantha Dizon)

⤜⤚⤜⤚

"Never make big decisions...
when you're in a bad place."
(Lori Halopoff-Fenelon)

❧❧❧

"Although the world is filled with suffering,
it is also filled with overcoming!"
(Helen Keller)
(Shared by Marcia Holman)

❧❧❧

"It's much more meaningful to do something
for free, because we <u>want</u> to...
than to get paid, to do the very same thing...
because we <u>have</u> to."

❧❧❧

"Appreciate often, how good you really have it,
no matter what! Be grateful... always!"

❧❧❧

"Concentrating too much on one thing will ensure that you are paying attention to it... but to the <u>detriment</u> of everything else."

࿆࿆࿆

"Flexibility in time of hardship, far outweighs being stuck on what you think life should be like."
(Teresa Cimino)

࿆࿆࿆

"Staying positive doesn't mean you have to be happy all the time. It means that even on hard days, you know that better ones are coming."
(Sarah Turner)

࿆࿆࿆

"One day at a time." *(Kirra Willert)*

࿆࿆࿆

true *kind* *necessary*

"Before you speak, let your words pass
through three gates: Is it true?
Is it necessary? Is it kind?" (Anon)
(Shared by Chrissie Casey-Brockman)

❧❧❧

"Life is like a rolling wheel... and no matter how
much you try, you can't always stay on top of it."
(Natalia Todorov)

❧❧❧

"Some of our favorite memories often involve incidents that seemed completely forgettable at the time... but mean 'the world' to us, all these years later."

❦❦❦

"The word, HIDEOUS, is one of my favorite words because of its hyperbolic and humorous overtones. It is a word that encapsulates the ridiculous, embarrassing and often heartfelt moments that one experiences in life. Laughter can always assuage the soul and that is what the word, HIDEOUS, does for me. In my world, it is a part of who I am because of its refreshing and anecdotal qualities. But unless a person really knows me... I always refrain from wishing them a perfectly HIDEOUS day! They probably wouldn't understand."

(Linda Atherton)

❦❦❦

*"Even when tired... you'd be astonished
at how much one can accomplish,
with the right mindset!"*

⁂

"To love another person is to see the face of God."
(Claude-Michel Schonberg & John Cameron)
(Shared by Keree James)

⁂

"Optimism is the best way to see life!"
(Anon)
(Shared by Janae West)

⁂

"Learn to rest, not to quit." *(Julianne Hunt)*

⁂

*"The best way to improve your
chances of finishing... is to start!"*

⁂

"If you believe you can...
you more than likely CAN!"
(Gene Nobles)

⚮⚮⚮

"Success is a by-product of excellence!"
(Alex Willert)

⚮⚮⚮

"The secret to avoiding getting caught-up
in the news 24/7... is to always have
something better to do."

⚮⚮⚮

"The search for truth has nothing to
do with what anyone else believes."

⚮⚮⚮

"Crying is human... but so is laughter!"

⚮⚮⚮

"As long as I dream of a better life... I will always have plenty of <u>preparation</u> to do!"

සිටිස

"Depression is living in the past, anxiety is living in the future... and happiness is living in the present."
(Alex Willert)

සිටිස

"When you are creating something, don't ever give up! Work through the process, no matter how long it takes! Even throwing away what seem like great ideas, is normal! If you stay the course... To the very end... You'll be satisfied!"
(Doug Kuhl)

සිටිස

"You've gotta listen... to hear!"

(Patricia A. Morris)

❧❧❧

"Fear does not stop death... it stops life.

And worrying does not take away

tomorrow's troubles...

it takes away today's peace."

(Anon)

(Shared by LuAnne Ponce Montilla)

❧❧❧

"Imagining it, is the first step...

in creating anything."

❧❧❧

"Accept what is, let go of what was...

and have faith in what will be."

(Sabrina Ganier)

❧❧❧

"Enjoy the little things,

for one day,

you may look back and realize...

they were the big things."

(Robert Brault)

(Shared by Jeanette Zapata)

❦❦❦

"It's all about having wisdom.

Some people talk a lot...

but really say nothing.

In contrast, other folks say very little...

but you can just tell...

it's important to take-in every word."

❦❦❦

"Sometimes all you need is a good nap!"

(Katie Willert)

❦❦❦

Chapter Three:
RANDOM OBSERVATIONS!

Random Observations, is the category that houses the broadest array of motivational sayings. Everything fits here, as long as it has purpose and is in some way… helpful. Random observations are usually designated to those which might embrace different viewpoints than the usual. This chapter is dedicated to a contributing author and wonderful friend, *Gene Nobles.* Gene has a real love for theatre and music and is a true supporter of the Brea Olinda choirs. He is generous, humble and very thoughtful. He greets each day with an inspiring combination of hope and joy. Gene has made it a point to attend the Brea Olinda High School choir concerts as often as he can, since the early 2000's, even though his grandkids stopped performing there in 2009! He has been, and is, without a doubt… the choir's greatest fan!

In his own words, he shares, *"I am surprised and truly honored to have Dave include me in his book. My family and I have been fortunate to have been so wonderfully entertained by Dave and his choirs for eleven years (2006-2016) and now his son, Alex, and the Brea choirs for the past four! I have always admired persons who spend their time and efforts to help others succeed. The author of this book and other teachers like him, are perfect examples of this! My wife, Jan, and I have enjoyed remembering many of the sayings and advice that may find their way into Dave's book. There is one, however, that we all know and also one that my parents repeated over and over to me when growing up. This is the same one I try to convey to all my family… and that is **The Golden Rule! Do unto others as you would have them do unto you**! If we all followed this one, how much better we all would be. Jan and I think Dave's newest book is a wonderful idea, and we are so looking forward to the results of his efforts! Thank you, Dave, for all of the inspiration we undoubtedly will be able to absorb from these writings. And to all of you readers, I hope the book will be of much delight and information for you. I wish you all good health, good fortune and much happiness!"*

Sincerely,

Gene Nobles

"If you try hard enough, you can always find something to like in everyone you meet."

(Gene Nobles)

∽∾∽∾∽

"Your imagination <u>expands</u> your reality!"

∽∾∽∾∽

*"Every time an old person dies,
it's like a library burning down."*
(Alex Haley)

∽∾∽∾∽∾

*"Sometimes the bad things that happen
in our lives put us directly on the path to
the best things that will ever happen to us!"*
(Anon)
(Shared by Linda Atherton)

∽∾∽∾∽∾

*"Life is a bland canvass, and you need
to throw all the paint on it you can!"*
(Danny Kaye)

∽∾∽∾∽∾

*"Those people who constantly complain and
threaten to quit things... probably should."*

∽∾∽∾∽∾

"A hasty achievement is usually a flawed one."

༄༅༄༅༄

"The fact that we want things... doesn't
necessarily mean we'll be happy
once we get them!"

༄༅༄༅༄

"No matter what you choose to do in life...
Make it beautiful!"

༄༅༄༅༄

"The more we love...
the more we <u>are</u> loved."

༄༅༄༅༄

"It's easier to build strong children,
than to repair broken men."
(Frederick Douglass)
(Shared by Natalia Todorov)

༄༅༄༅༄

"An actor who performs a small role with all that he can muster, is a thousand times more valuable than the actor who feels entitled to play <u>only</u> the lead parts. This is because the value of an actor is not defined by the <u>roles</u> he plays, but rather by the <u>heart</u> he instills... into each role he plays!"

(Anon)

❧❧❧

"A life of gratitude starts with a single grateful thought... and then another... and another..."

(Elizabeth Rose)

(Shared by Jeanette Zapata)

❧❧❧

"It's always easier to laugh... if you smile first."

❧❧❧

*"Everyone makes mistakes in life, but that
doesn't mean they have to pay for them
for the rest of their life. Sometimes
good people make bad choices.
It doesn't mean they're bad...
it means they're human."*
(Anon)
(Shared by Douglas Newton)

❦

*"Whenever you don't seem to fit-in with the other
people around you, don't get depressed...
instead, thank God for the wonderful
uniqueness you possess, and
spend some time searching
for your proper niche."*

❦

"To be most successful... be content and happy."

❦

*"Many people only consider believing
things that have already been proven true.
What fun is there in that?"*

∽∽∽

*"No one is more hated than he
who speaks the truth."* (Plato)

∽∽∽

*"Of all the wonderful gifts we each are
blessed with, I would place 'to laugh'
and 'to love'... at the very top of my list."*

∽∽∽

*"The butterfly does not look back at the
caterpillar in shame, just as you should
not look back at your past in shame. Your
past was part of your own transformation."*
(Anon) (Marcia Holman)

∽∽∽

"Just because I disagree with you,
does not mean that I hate you.
We need to relearn that in society."
(Anon)
(Shared by Douglas Newton)

❧❧❧

"There is more than enough hope for
all of us if we only put our faith into it."

❧❧❧

"Cherish yourself, and surround yourself with
those who see in you the incomparable light
of your being. See who brings out kinder,
gentler, more beautiful qualities in you.
Let them be the people in your boat!"
(Omid Safi)
(Shared by Jeanette Zapata)

❧❧❧

"We all have dreams we long to reach,
yet often, after we do… we're dissatisfied?
Every dream is not equal. Perhaps we
should have aimed higher and
challenged ourselves more
from the very start?
Luckily, it's never too late to
adjust our dreams…
and try again!"

∽∽∽

"Don't dwell on negative stuff unless you want to
become negative. As Buddha once said,
'We are, what we think.'"
(Inspired by Buddha)

∽∽∽

"Just because someone carries it well…
doesn't mean it isn't heavy."
(Anon) (Natalia Todorov)

∽∽∽

"No matter what is happening...

'This too shall pass!'"

(Anon)

(Shared by Della Long)

❧❧❧

"To lead an orchestra... sometimes you

have to turn your back on the crowd."

(Jerry Halpin)

❧❧❧

"A good leader encourages and leads by example, while a poor leader... <u>doesn't</u>!"

⌘⌘⌘

"Never get into a pissing contest with your boss."
(Carl Nielsen) (Shared by Kurt Nielsen)

⌘⌘⌘

"Love means never having to say you're sorry... but doing it anyway."

⌘⌘⌘

"Never stop listening to the song of a kind and happy person. Learn to sing along with them in perfect harmony!"

⌘⌘⌘

"Don't blame the world when something goes awry. Blame yourself if you're not concerned about fixing it!"

⌘⌘⌘

"If you can't do what you do…
do what you can."
(Jon Bon Jovi)
(Shared by Jennifer Zamora)

***

"When I'm about to perform in front of people
and I begin to feel nervous… I remind myself
of a quote from the movie, Sister Act II:
'Never mind how you feel. Think about how
you're gonna make <u>them</u> feel!'"
(Whoopi Goldberg)
(Shared by Claire Manson)

***

"If you're not doing things you want to
be doing, or spending time with those
you love… then just know…
it's never too late to start!"

***

*"Change for the sake of change is like a
bell that never stops ringing. At first it
holds your attention... but soon, after
you realize that the pitch never varies,
it grows very tiresome, until finally...
it dawns on you... you're listening to
a great big, irritating waste of time!"*

❧❧❧

*"When we spend our lives with people
we love, we tend to smile a lot...
and time goes by so much faster!"*

❧❧❧

*"Most of us may have a lot of acquaintances,
but only a few really close friends.
Remember to nurture every
good friendship, you have,
because ultimately... it's worth it!"*

❧❧❧

"Thinking deep and wise thoughts...
is not the same as <u>sharing</u> them with others!"

⟡⟡⟡⟡

"It's easier for most people to complain than
to do something about it!" (Vangie Obrero)

⟡⟡⟡⟡

"We don't always have the power to make
good things happen for every situation.
But once in a while, when we really
need it, something truly miraculous
presents itself... out of nowhere!"

⟡⟡⟡⟡

"People who spend a lot of time alone are not
necessarily unhappy or even unsociable.
In their world, at times, they may just
prefer the sound of silence to think,
to create or to recharge."

⟡⟡⟡⟡

"Often, disappointment, in an unexpected way,
actually serves as a precursor...
to success!"

⸎⸎⸎

"Unfortunately, love is not always mutual,
and there's absolutely nothing anyone
can do about it... except... to accept it!"

⸎⸎⸎

"It's wonderful how sometimes a person
we have just met... can quickly
feel like an old friend."

⸎⸎⸎

"My bed is a magical place,
where I suddenly remember...
everything I forgot to do today!"
(Anon)
(Shared by Marcia Holman)

⸎⸎⸎

"Everybody is a genius; but if you judge a fish by its ability to climb a tree, it will live its whole life thinking it is stupid."

(Julie Andrews)

(Shared by Chrysti B. Lajoie)

"As gratitude goes up... anxiety goes down."
(Pastor Gene Appel) (Shared by Lauren Poling)

❧❧❧

"You see, the truth so many people seem to miss is that happiness doesn't start with a relationship, education or college degree. It starts with your thoughts, and what you tell yourself every day!" *(Anon)*
(Shared by Natalia Todorov)

❧❧❧

"If you ever wonder where God resides? Look deeply into the inquisitive and loving eyes of a baby!"

❧❧❧

"The world is our playground, and life... is our teacher."

❧❧❧

"Negativity serves an important purpose.
It's the comparison mindset that makes
being positive... so much more appealing!"

❧❧❧

"Promise only what you can deliver...
then deliver more than you promise."
(Anon) (Shared by Jeanette Zapata)

❧❧❧

"Life is about giving, of course...
but it's also about graciously
receiving from others!"

❧❧❧

"Do everything with a good heart
and expect nothing in return...
and you will never be disappointed."
(Anon)
(Shared by Rita Jones)

❧❧❧

"Watching people helping others, even in small ways, feels right... but not as right as when that person is <u>you</u>!"

❦❦❦

"It's funny about life, once you begin to take note of the things you are grateful for... you begin to lose sight of the things you lack."

(Germany Kent)

(Shared by Claire Manson)

❦❦❦

"Our lives are like mazes, that are constantly changing, forcing us to always adapt and never get too comfortable. But then at the same time... that's what makes each of our lives such an adventure!"

❦❦❦

"I wouldn't trade our great friendship
for anything... not even a better one!
What am I saying?
There could never be a <u>better</u> one!"

⌘⌘⌘

"If you are the smartest person in the room...
then you are in the wrong room."
(Confucius)
(Shared by Natalia Todorov)

⌘⌘⌘

"It's fascinating how every day, each
of us continues to create our own
personal stories through what we think,
do and say. Who needs television! Life
provides us with plenty of entertainment
through living and watching others...
who are doing exactly the same thing!"

⌘⌘⌘

"Don't ever feel embarrassed to ask one of your loved ones for a hug. How else would they know that you needed one?"

❧❧❧

"Always appreciate those people who contribute toward your happiness in life... and don't forget to reciprocate!"

❧❧❧

"One who is singing... does not have ill thoughts toward others."
(Bulgarian proverb)
(Shared by Natalia Todorov)

❧❧❧

"Just because you think differently than a lot of other people... does not mean that your words should not be respected."

❧❧❧

*"A huge recipe for regret is the feeling that
you could have done something better...
but you ran out of time to fix it."*

❦❦❦

*"A full life is about having a plethora
of experiences and achievements;
some not as great as others...
but all ultimately leading
us to happiness."*

❦❦❦

*"The best way to deal with a bad situation,
is not so much about fixing it...
as working to build a better one!"*
(Paraphrased words of Socrates)

❦❦❦

*"One good friend is all you need... but there's
no rule that says you can't have more."*

❦❦❦

"Our lives are ever changing, but our fondest memories will burn bright in our minds for the rest of our lives... no matter how drastically things might change around us."

∽∂∽∂∽∂

"Reputation is what other people know about you... Honor is what you know about yourself."
(Lois Mcbride Bujold)
(Shared by Marcia Holman)

∽∂∽∂∽∂

"Being a good parent doesn't mean knowing where your kids are at all times... but having the confidence to know that wherever they are... they're doing well!"
(Yvette Hernandez)

∽∂∽∂∽∂

"It's not all or nothing... it's all or something."

(Debbie Lee)

"Not all of us are dealt the right cards, but that doesn't mean you can't reshuffle the deck... for a better outcome."
(Anon)
(Shared by Tassa Hampton-Varga)

⁓⁓⁓

"It's not the breaths you take... but the moments that take your breath away."
(Catherine Rhodes)

⁓⁓⁓

"Happiness is a place between too much and too little."
(Anon)

⁓⁓⁓

"Lies can be just as strongly believed as truth!"

⁓⁓⁓

*"Whenever I write something to be
published, first, I always make sure that
I enjoyed reading it, myself. That gives me
the confidence that no matter what...
at least one person liked it!"*

❧❧❧

*"We basically create our own lives through
how we adapt to everything that happens
to us, which goals we choose to pursue
and our levels of tenacity. So, if we
are unhappy with any part of that...
we know who to take it up with!"*

❧❧❧

*"I believe we demonstrate the best of ourselves
when we are willing to stand-up for what
we believe in, regardless of how popular
that stand is... and worst...
when we just quietly sit on our hands."*

❧❧❧

"If excuses were dollars... we'd all be rich!"

❦❦❦

"Initially, we cease feeling self-confident the moment we believe that what we are doing, doesn't seem important to anyone else. But we regain that confidence, just as soon as we realize... that it's <u>our</u> opinion, not theirs... that matters most here!"

❦❦❦

"The big don't eat the small... the fast eat the slow."
(Carlos Morales)

❦❦❦

"If the devil can't make you bad, he will surely make you busy!"
(Annette Ambrose-Schumann)

❦❦❦

*"To me, a beautiful day has little
to do with the weather."*

❧❧❧

*"Our lives, like a river, sometimes suffer
through droughts, but ultimately...
we just keep rolling along!"*

❧❧❧

*"I have heard it said, that 'nothing we
do really matters,' but turns to dust
once we pass away. I disagree. I
believe that everything we do, that
somehow affects others for better
or for worse... matters a lot!"*

❧❧❧

*"You always pass failure...
on the way to success!"*
(Mickey Rooney)

❧❧❧

"As soon as you concern yourself with the 'good' and the 'bad' of your fellows, you create an opening in your heart for the maliciousness to enter. Testing, competing with and criticizing others, weakens and defeats you."

(Morihei Ueshiba)

(Shared by Natalia Todorov)

❧❧❧

"Feeling sad goes all the way down to the bottom of the soul... but fortunately... so does feeling happy!"

❧❧❧

"Although some people may vehemently insist that their way is the best way... I still believe that we are required, as intelligent human beings... to always decide for ourselves!"

❧❧❧

"Everything comes to pass, and nothing
comes to stay... but Jesus does!"
(Stan Knight)

❧❧❧❧

"Don't jump from A to Z.
Remember, there are 24
other letters in the alphabet!"
(Keree James)

❧❧❧❧

"Due to the unpredictable duration of each
of our lives, grudge holding and ill will are
less than pointless. On the other hand, it's
a great time for sincere hugs and smiles!"

❧❧❧❧

"The truth can be ugly... but beautiful
and freeing, all at the same time."
(Vangie Obrero)

❧❧❧❧

*"If your education doesn't get you
where you want to go... try your wits!"*

⌘⌘⌘

*"Only a life lived for others...
is a life worthwhile."*
(Albert Einstein)

⌘⌘⌘

*"When you've done something wrong,
admit it and be sorry. No one in
history has ever choked to death
from swallowing his pride."*
(Anon) (Shared by Douglas Newton)

⌘⌘⌘

*"It takes determination and
practice, practice, practice...
to learn something new."*
(Teresa Cimino)

⌘⌘⌘

"Life is made-up of seasons and choices."
(Kathleen Scott-Kay)

❧❧❧

"Happiness is a state of mind. It's just according to how you look at things."
(Walt Disney)

❧❧❧

"Showing kindness... melts even
the iciest of hearts."

❧❧❧

"It's always good to <u>strive</u> for the best,
but never to <u>expect</u> the best or the worst.
Life is normally somewhere in-between.
If you think, in this way, you will always
be in a better place...
to handle <u>whatever</u> happens!"

❧❧❧

"People who win through cheating...
really don't win at all!"

❧❧❧

"So many people wish they could just snap
their fingers and become successful!
I, for one, get much more satisfaction...
by earning it!"

❧❧❧

"Hope is there... long after everything else has failed."

☙❧☙❧

"So many people from the past, know a version of you... that doesn't exist anymore."
(Tassa Hampton-Varga)

☙❧☙❧

"If you aren't getting anywhere, going around in circles... why not try being a <u>tangent</u> for a while?"

☙❧☙❧

"Being negative only makes a difficult journey more difficult. You may be given a cactus... but you don't have to sit on it!"
(Joyce Meyer)
(Shared by Marcia Holman)

☙❧☙❧

"When you aren't controlling your own thoughts, no one really knows who you are... not even you!"

✇✇✇

"Piling degrading jokes and criticisms onto someone, when they're down, is probably not how we would wish to be treated... under similar circumstances."

✇✇✇

"Fear begets more fear, but courage... begets confidence!"

✇✇✇

"Do all the good you can, and make as little fuss as possible."
(Charles Dickens)
(Shared by Jeanette Zapata)

✇✇✇

"The loudest and most passionate voice in the room is not always right for every situation that arises. Sometimes, it behooves us to listen to those quietly and calmly... speaking in the corner."

❧❧❧

"Sometimes our very best friends are the ones we never knew we had... until we really needed them!"

❧❧❧

"The biggest challenge facing anyone with a creative mind, is finding a way to make practical use of their ideas, talents and accomplishments. But there's always one perfect solution... if they are only tenacious enough to keep looking for it!"

❧❧❧

"In life, successfully adapting to surprise changes, that come your way, is far more helpful than complaining."

❧❧❧

"Sometimes, walking away has nothing to do with weakness... and everything to do with strength."
(Sabrina Ganier)

❧❧❧

"Just as soon as you can imagine living a better life, there is absolutely nothing stopping you from pursuing it... except maybe your own excuses and fears."

❧❧❧

"Life is really simple, but we insist on making it complicated."
(Confucius)

❧❧❧

"The person who created winners and losers, probably didn't foresee it bleeding into politics. I like it when people work together through their differences, creating compromises that work for everyone. It just feels right. We don't see examples of that in the world much anymore... but in my opinion, that doesn't make compromise outdated... just underused."

⚬⚬⚬⚬

"It's no use going back to yesterday, because I was a different person then."
(Lewis Carroll from Alice In Wonderland)
(Shared by Doug Newton)

⚬⚬⚬⚬

"There's much more to life than meets the eye... if we just open up our other one!"

⚬⚬⚬⚬

"People are like stained glass windows.
They sparkle and shine when the sun is out,
but when the darkness sets in,
their true beauty is revealed only...
if there is a light from within."
(Elisabeth Kubler-Ross)
(Shared by Jeanette Zapata)

⸐⸑⸐⸑⸐⸑

"Coincidence is God's way of remaining anonymous."
(Albert Einstein)

⸐⸑⸐⸑⸐⸑

"Instead of buying your children all the things
you never had... you should teach them all
the things you were never taught. Material
wears out, but knowledge stays!"
(Bruce Lee)
(Shared by Marcia Holman)

⸐⸑⸐⸑⸐⸑

"All the adversity I've had in my life, all my troubles and obstacles, have strengthened me. You may not realize it when it happens, but a kick in the teeth may be... the best thing in the world for you!"
(Walt Disney)

✎✎✎✎

*"People pleasers are slaves to their own need for approval, while independent thinkers are always targets from dissenting minds.
Pick your poison!"*

✎✎✎✎

"I don't really enjoy reading little motivational sayings... I much prefer the bigger ones!"

✎✎✎✎

"I would rather die of passion, than of boredom!"
(Vincent van Gogh)

✎✎✎✎

"For every set-back we experience,
there is a potential 'success story'
out there... just waiting for
us to embrace."

❧❧❧

"Try to be a rainbow in someone else's cloud!"
(Amaya Angelou)
(Shared by Marcia Holman)

❧❧❧

"Being tenaciously inquisitive,
always leads to questions,
which in time... will lead to answers!"

❧❧❧

"Just as soon as you decide the
excitement in your life is gone...
it's about time to start
a new adventure!"

❧❧❧

"Some things break your heart...
but fix your vision." (Anon)
(Shared by Douglas Newton)

❧❧❧

"As much as patience is considered a virtue,
the lack of it... is definitely not!"

❧❧❧

"Hate, it has caused a lot of problems
in the world... but has not
solved one yet."
(Maya Angelou)
(Shared by Natalia Todorov)

❧❧❧

"A nation is like a tree. It has many branches
that grow in different directions, but as long
as the roots are healthy... the tree is strong!"
(Natalia Todorov)

❧❧❧

"Always look on the bright side of life!"
(Monty Python)

❧❧❧

"To me, love does not always culminate in a
passionate embrace, like in the movies.
It's just the opposite. Love cares deeply,
but gets cranky sometimes.
Love can be passionate,
but is more often controlled.
Movie passion is fine...
but I prefer my love to be the real thing!"

❧❧❧

"Even before understanding our differences,
it's easy to assume that anyone who
thinks differently from us is wrong...
because, let's face it...
No one likes being on the <u>losing</u> side
of anything!"

❧❧❧

"I have wept in the night,

For the shortness of sight,

That to somebody's need made me blind.

But I never have yet,

Felt a tinge of regret,

For being a little too kind."

(Thomas S. Monson)

(Shared by Linda Atherton)

❧❧❧

"Someone is out there holding their breath,

waiting for you to fail...

Make sure they suffocate."

(Anon) (Shared by Douglas Newton)

❧❧❧

"When you lose your way, taking stock of your

life through comprehending what is most

and least important to you... is a great

way to get yourself back on track!"

❧❧❧

"The principal part of faith... is patience."

(George MacDonald)

(Shared by Jeanette Zapata)

❧❧❧

"Everyone we know who is truly kind, friendly and thoughtful is a person we should appreciate. But more importantly... we should emulate."

❧❧❧

"Courage is not 'having the strength to go on;' it is 'going on when you don't have the strength.'"

(Theodore Roosevelt)

(Shared by Dina, Michelle & Jon Willert)

❧❧❧

"A book full of useful information is only helpful... if it's read!"

❧❧❧

*"No one should expect the magic of Christmas
to solve all of the world's problems...
It just provides a blueprint to try."*

∽∞∽∞∽∞

*"When you know you are loved...
it's one of the nicest feelings in the world!"*

∽∞∽∞∽∞

*"I think as you grow older
your Christmas list gets shorter,
because the things you want...
can't be bought."*
(By John Tesh)
(Shared by Linda Atherton)

∽∞∽∞∽∞

*"There is only one way to
fail at a project...
but a <u>myriad</u> of ways to succeed!"*

∽∞∽∞∽∞

"Your presence is present enough."

(Lori Halopoff-Fenelon)

❧❧❧

"Life is like a pizza...
It's all about the flavor of the toppings."

❧❧❧

"The older I get, the more excited I am
about the gifts I give...
and the less picky I am about
the gifts I receive."

❧❧❧

"There is one thing that is most important...
being right with your creator.
Whether you call it religious
or self-aware...
It is what it is."

(Tassa Hampton-Varga)

❧❧❧

"Don't worry.
If it was that important…
you would have brought it with you."
(Laura Ann Washington-Franklin)

✥

"It's so much easier to take risks, once you
stop focusing on what you could lose…
and focus instead on just how
much you have to gain!"

✥

"When 'I' is replaced with 'we,'
even illness becomes wellness."
(Malcolm X)
(Shared by Natalia Todorov)

✥

"Happiness, unlike success…
is all about balance."

✥

"If you are a sensitive person, who cries over happy endings, don't feel embarrassed... feel lucky!"

❧❧❧

"When all else fails... laugh!"

❧❧❧

*"Don't fear death. When it comes, let
your life stand, as a testament to others,
that love, forgiveness, integrity,
hope, truth, faith and compassion...
are the parts that really matter."*

⚬⚬⚬⚬⚬

*"There was never a good war
or a bad peace."*
(Benjamin Franklin)

⚬⚬⚬⚬⚬

*"A year should be seen as much more
than merely 365 days on the calendar...
It should be seen as 365 glorious opportunities
for each of us to make the most of!"*
(Anon)

⚬⚬⚬⚬⚬

"Life is but happiness and time." (James Willert)

⚬⚬⚬⚬⚬

"In N Out, cures all! It's good for the soul."
(Katie Willert)

⌘

"Remember when Chicken Little ran around screaming, 'The sky is falling,' causing everyone else to do the same? Well… it wasn't."

⌘

"While two people are arguing… a third one always wins."
(Bulgarian proverb)
(Shared by Natalia Todorov)

⌘

"We spend much of our lives trying to fit-in with everyone else, not realizing that our greatest gift… is our uniqueness!"

⌘

"In times like these, hold on to your faith, be kind to others and ride this life until the wheels fall off. None of us are getting out of life alive. Enjoy the ride."
(Tassa Hampton-Varga)

⋞⋟⋞⋟⋞⋟

"Whether something is seen as right or wrong usually depends on your point of view. But don't be afraid to question that point of view from time to time... People __do__ change their minds."

⋞⋟⋞⋟⋞⋟

"I had an inheritance from my Father, it was the Moon and the Sun. And though I roam all over the world, the spending of it is never done."
(Ernest Hemingway)
(Shared by Marcia Holman)

⋞⋟⋞⋟⋞⋟

"We can't control life... but we can always adapt!"

⁓⁓⁓⁓

"Growing old is mandatory,
but growing up... is optional."
(Walt Disney)

⁓⁓⁓⁓

"I know we change through the experiences
we endure over the years, but with
any luck, whatever our best
qualities were as a child...
they will still be there as an adult."

⁓⁓⁓⁓

"The art of happiness lies in
the power of <u>extracting</u>
happiness from common things."
(Henry Ward Beecher)
(Shared by Jeanette Zapata)

⁓⁓⁓⁓

*"I believe 'right' always wins in the end...
although it seldom follows anyone's
expected timeline."*

❦❦❦

*"Happiness. Tragedy.
Both happen when you least expect them."*
(Anon)
(paraphrased by Kathy Walborn)

❦❦❦

*"Take the time to wish happy thoughts to your
loved ones... and then to everybody else.
Good things result from sharing our
blessings with everyone!"*

❦❦❦

"If you stumble... make it part of the dance."
(Anon)

❦❦❦

"I hope there are days when your coffee tastes like magic, your playlist makes you dance, strangers make you smile and the night sky touches your soul. I hope you fall in love with being alive again."

(Anon)

(Shared by Natalia Todorov)

∽∽∽∽

"It may be difficult dealing with judgmental people, but ignoring their hurtful words... may be a very good place to start."

∽∽∽∽

"In times of stress, an extreme mentality usually doesn't lead to the best course of action. Excessive panic or disregard are foolish. Instead, stay calm, think rationally... and make sensible decisions."

(Erin Garcia)

∽∽∽∽

"There's nothing like a
comfortable pair of old shoes."
(Frances Nielsen)
(Shared by Kurt Nielsen)

⚬⚬⚬⚬⚬⚬

"From caring comes courage."
(Lao Tzu)
(Shared by Vangie Obrero)

⚬⚬⚬⚬⚬⚬

"I believe that some of our best ideas
may come to us while daydreaming,
only to be forgotten, moments later.
But, rest assured, <u>we were brilliant</u>...
if only for a moment."

⚬⚬⚬⚬⚬⚬

"If you gave a party and nobody came...
No problem... More ice cream and cake for you!"

⚬⚬⚬⚬⚬⚬

"Anxiety happens when you think you have to figure out everything all at once. Breathe. You're strong. You got this. Take it day by day."

(Karen Salmansohn)

(Shared by Stephanie Miller)

"Interpretation is not the truth...
It's a creative art!"

∽⌒∽⌒∽

"The smallest act of kindness is worth
more than the greatest intention."
(Kahlil Gibran)
(Shared by Jeanette Zapata)

∽⌒∽⌒∽

"A number of people I've known, end friendships
by not responding to texts or phone calls.
They probably feel that this inaction puts them
on the moral high ground. But I think they
are just angry... and content to stay that way."

∽⌒∽⌒∽

"The simplest solution is most likely the right one."
(Occam's razor by William of Occam)
(Shared by Alex Willert)

∽⌒∽⌒∽

"Movement is life... keep on moving!"
(Eddie Sibal)

❧❧❧

"The world will not be destroyed by those who do evil... but by those who <u>watch</u> them without doing anything."
(Albert Einstein)
(Shared by Douglas Newton)

❧❧❧

**"Life is so unpredictable...
Adapt well... and flourish!"**

❧❧❧

"The two most important days in your life are the day you are born... and the day you find out why!"
(Mark Twain)
(Shared by Marcia Holman)

❧❧❧

*"Reminiscing about a wonderful past is fine...
as long as you don't forget about
pursuing your potentially better future."*

❧

*"Try __not__ to bolster your confidence by
looking for people who agree with you.
Bolster your confidence...
by __believing__ in yourself!"*

❧

*"If you want to know who controls you...
look at who you are not allowed to criticize."*
(Voltaire)
(Shared by Justin Senneff)

❧

"Music can cure things medication never will."
(Anon) (Shared by Teresa Cimino)

❧

181

*"Those we love don't go away...
they walk beside us every day."*
(Anon)
(Shared by Natalia Todorov)

ꞔꞔꞔ

**"To travel from wildly emotional reactions
to current events, to calmly seeing the
whole picture...
is the gift we receive when
we are patient."**

ꞔꞔꞔ

**"When we think like we did as children,
we regain that uncanny power
to transform any day,
no matter how ordinary...
into an extraordinarily
fun adventure!"**

ꞔꞔꞔ

"Go to Heaven for the climate...
Hell, for the company."
(Mark Twain)

❧❧❧

"Life without imagination...
is pretty darn dull.
Variety is the spice of life!"
(Anon)

❧❧❧

"In life, there is really nothing
permanent to build on...
except truth and hope and love."

❧❧❧

"When everything seems to be going against you,
remember that the airplane takes off
against the wind... not with it."
(Henry Ford) (Shared by Marcia Holman)

❧❧❧

"I still remember when I prayed
for the things I have now."
(Anna Clarke)
(Shared by Coleen Caron)

❧❧❧

"If you're green, you grow,
but if you're brown... you rot."
(Anon) (Shared by Troy Peace)

❧❧❧

"Being mean is the weak person's
interpretation of being strong!"
(Ed Mylett)
(Shared by Chrysti B. Lajoie)

❧❧❧

"People who feel they are doing the world
a favor by sharing their hateful views...
definitely are not!"

❧❧❧

"Feeling stressed about everyday problems is unnecessary. For your own peace of mind... learn to chill... and roll with each new day's surprises!"

ᑲᑲᑲᑲ

"As far as possible, without surrender, be on good terms with all persons. Speak your truth quietly and clearly. Enjoy your achievements as well as your plans. Keep interested in your own career, however humble. Be yourself. Beyond a wholesome discipline, be gentle with yourself. You are a child of the universe."
(excerpts from Desiderata, 1692)
(Shared by Marti Repp)

ᑲᑲᑲᑲ

"Truth cannot be confirmed by rumors."

ᑲᑲᑲᑲ

**"Life is just a bowl of cherries. Don't take it serious,
it's mysterious. Life is just a bowl of cherries,
so live and laugh and laugh at love...
love a laugh, laugh and love."** *(Bob Fosse)*

"Stay away from negative people...
They have a problem for every solution!"
(Albert Einstein)
(Shared by Marcia Holman)

∽∂∽∂∽∂

"Not everyone believes what we do is exceptional.
Sometimes their critical opinions may even
cause us to fall short of reaching our goals
or to feel badly. But no matter who these
people are, their beliefs don't necessarily
mean we're on the wrong track...
nor should they ever cause us
to stop believing in ourselves."

∽∂∽∂∽∂

"Being busy and getting a lot done, in the
process, is great! But to me, sitting
at home with my family, laughing
at nothing in particular... is better!"

∽∂∽∂∽∂

"A man of words and not of deeds,
is like a garden full of weeds."
(Percy B. Green)
(Shared by Natalia Todorov)

⌘⌘⌘

**"The joy of creating something from
the heart, doesn't end upon successful
completion of the project. It ends once
we 'cease' to fondly remember the entire
process... which of course, will never
happen... as long as we live!"**

⌘⌘⌘

**"I have learned through bitter experience
the one supreme lesson, to conserve my anger
as heat conserved, is transmuted into energy.
Even so, our anger controlled can be
transmuted into a power which
can move the world."** *(Gandhi)*

⌘⌘⌘

"To stay positive, always project that what's coming... is better than what is gone!"
(Jenevieve M. Fuentes)

❧❦❧

"Growing up is mandatory... being old, is an attitude."
(Natalia Todorov)

❧❦❧

"Good music that reflects our emotions, once heard... is never forgotten."

❧❦❧

"The person with the highest IQ... is not always the lead singer in the band."

❧❦❧

"Instead of being bored... be imaginative!"

❧❦❧

*"I don't trust anyone who's nice to me,
but rude to the waiter, because they
would treat me the same way,
if I were in that position."*
(Muhammad Ali)

❧❧❧

*"Did you change... or did you just
stop being who you are not?"*
(Susie Harriger)
(Shared by Douglas Newton)

❧❧❧

*"The cake always tastes better when
the baker takes pride in their work!"*

❧❧❧

*"You're going to be happy, said life...
but first, I'll make you strong!"*
(Sabrina Ganier)

❧❧❧

"Happiness is a byproduct of
feeling super-bitchin!"
(Anon)

❧❧❧

"I pray you heal from things no
one ever apologized for."
(Anon)
(Shared by Marylen Ayash-Borgen)

❧❧❧

"Freedom is the oxygen of the soul."
(Moshe Dayan)
(Shared by Chrysti B. Lajoie)

❧❧❧

"When you allow a family member or
friend to go on feeling depressed,
with no real effort to help...
you become part of the problem."

❧❧❧

191

"When we truly respect someone, years after
we have last seen them, whether they were
our parent, sibling, teacher, pastor, neighbor,
coworker, role model or friend, we
'absolutely know,' they inspired us!
Not because the world told us to feel that way...
but because we can't help but remember WHY
they deserve to be so honored. And, because of
the lasting positive influence they made, not
only on our lives... but through us...
on the lives of our children."

~~~~~

"The way to deal with a crisis is to keep your
wits about you and keep your life as
normal as possible. Your life has
not ended, so make sure you don't
act like it has. Find reasons to
smile and laugh
every day!"

~~~~~

"In junior high, I was challenged to a fight after school for my first and only time ever! Although my pride made me accept, I was frightfully nervous all day long. When the arranged time finally arrived for the 'big fight'... I actually won... because the other guy never showed up! Sometimes, threats ring hollow and you might just consider... calling their bluff!"

❧❧❧

"Never change, to be accepted by others. Stay weird!" (Anon)

❧❧❧

"Speak less than you know; have more than you show." (William Shakespeare)

❧❧❧

"Great minds DON'T always think alike!"

❧❧❧

"He that lies down with dogs...

shall rise up with fleas!"

(Benjamin Franklin)

✐✐✐✐✐

"Boys are boys... some are meaningful,

but some are just distractions in life."

(Coco James- age 10)

✐✐✐✐✐

"Stay open-minded. Sometimes, what you consider to be a mistake, may actually be seen by others... as genius!"

✺✺✺✺

"Fun is good!"
(Dr. Seuss)
(Shared by Douglas Newton)

✺✺✺✺

"Anyone who sees difficult times as a test of faith... is right!"

✺✺✺✺

"Don't coddle bad feelings. They'll feel at home and never leave you!"
(Betty Gardea)

✺✺✺✺

"Everything shiny is not gold."

✺✺✺✺

***"Stop living in your history
and live in your destiny!"***
(Brendan Burchard)
(Shared by Laura Ann Washington-Franklin)

❧❧❧

"Love, is the gift that keeps on giving!"
(Amy Wells)

❧❧❧

***"It always seems impossible...
until it's done!"***
(Nelson Mandela)

❧❧❧

***"You can't stop the water from boiling, when
there is a hot fire burning beneath it. Likewise,
when dealing with any sort of bias or unfairness
in your life, you can't stop your blood...
from doing the very same thing!"***

❧❧❧

"Always take your time with important decisions. Sometimes, when you hurriedly make a big decision, that affects a lot of people, and then later, after realizing it was actually a <u>bad</u> decision, you change your mind in an attempt to save face... don't be surprised if the only face looking for redemption... has EGG on it!"

⌘⌘⌘

"The definition of great leadership... begins with transparency."
(Robert Willert)

⌘⌘⌘

"Once we first realize, that some of our strongest beliefs may have actually been 'instilled' in us, through the years, by others? Perhaps we should 'revisit' each of those beliefs... just to be sure... they are <u>still</u> a good fit."

⌘⌘⌘

"Life's short... eat dessert first!"
(Melinda Nielsen)
(Shared by Kurt Nielsen)

છબછબછબ

"The moment you stop caring about or trying to succeed at something 'beautiful' in your life, that part of you... has died."

છબછબછબ

"One simple, kind and honest person is worth a thousand successful, charming, but <u>dishonest</u> liars!"

છબછબછબ

"The best achievements are done without fanfare or high expectations from others. They are achievements borne of hard work and passion, where what others think... just doesn't matter!"

છબછબછબ

"Motivation, not raw talent...
will <u>always</u> win in the end."

❦❦❦

"Happiness is not about getting all you
want... it is about <u>enjoying</u> all you have."
(Anon) (Shared by Linda Atherton)

❦❦❦

"When I was young, I always wished I could fly
through the air, like Superman! I grew up, fell
in love, got married, had a family and got to
know a lot of wonderful people. My life has been
great! As I look back on it, now, in a strange
way... I believe I really did get my wish!"

❦❦❦

"Do unto others as you would
have them do unto you."
(The Golden Rule)

❦❦❦

"Your life's journey is a never-ending process. Throughout your travels, recognize the impact of your thoughts, words and actions and be mindful and thoughtful with your decisions. Remember that you have the freedom and power of choice, and with that... comes responsibility."
(Lysa Gamboa-Levy)

❦❦❦

"Being smart is less about having the answers... and more about having the 'ability' to solve the questions."
(Alex Willert)

❦❦❦

"I've learned that people will forget what you said, people will forget what you did... but people will never forget how you made them feel." *(Maya Angelou)*
(Shared by Catherine Foley)

❦❦❦

Chapter Four:
HUMOROUS THOUGHTS!

I added the '*Humorous Thoughts*' Chapter at the end of this book, because it was suggested to me that no matter how much good food is served at a meal... it always needs a great dessert to top it off! So, here it is! This chapter is dedicated to a wonderful friend and contributing author, *John South*. John, a very funny guy, was our next-door neighbor for years, and was always the first to volunteer help, to anyone in need! His kind heart combined with his great desire and ability to achieve things, his incessant wit and his nonstop zest for life, was inspiring to everyone around him, including his wife, Annie and their two wonderful children, Kelsey and Daniel. As *Annie*, lovingly observed, *"He loved and appreciated life and nature to its fullest. He took nothing for granted."* Of course, that is all very true, but I'd also like to add that John possessed a natural sense of humor, which he shared freely, every day, helping each of us with the good fortune of knowing him, to smile and laugh, no matter how difficult our days had been! There was so much sincere and <u>infectious</u> joy in John, something that inspires me to this day! And truth be told... it is something that I... and anyone who really knew him... will <u>always</u> remember with a smile!

In Memory of *John South*

"Remember to find and relish the humor in your life."

(John South) (Shared by Annie South)

"The early bird catches the worm...
but who wants a worm!"
(Doug Kuhl)

✂︎✂︎✂︎

"When you really want to slap someone...
do it, and yell, 'mosquito!'" *(Anon)*
(Shared by Tami Seaton)

✂︎✂︎✂︎

"You can get much farther with a kind word and
a gun than you can with a kind word alone."
(Al Capone)
(Shared by Chris Breyer)

✂︎✂︎✂︎

"One big difference between a man a woman
is that when a woman says, 'Smell this,'...
it usually smells nice!" *(Anon)*
(Shared by Lizabeth Guichard)

✂︎✂︎✂︎

"Constantly criticizing other people seems
like a lame way to use our valuable time.
Why not just move on...
and find a reason
to <u>laugh</u> at them instead."

∽∾∽∾∽∾

"You know you're not someone's favorite,
when they come over to visit, take one
long look around the room,
and suddenly pause...
before staring blankly at you,
and asking, 'Isn't anybody here?'"

∽∾∽∾∽∾

"People cheating on their taxes disgust me!
This is not the world I want to raise
my 23 dependents in!"
(Anon)
(Shared by Laura Isbell)

∽∾∽∾∽∾

"After eating all of these Girl Scout cookies, my goal weight... is one chin."
(Vangie Obrero)

❧❧❧

"Television has brought back murder into the home... where it belongs."
(Alfred Hitchcock)

❧❧❧

"A computer once beat me at chess, but it was no match for me at kick boxing!"
(Emo Phillips)

❧❧❧

"Have you ever noticed that anybody driving slower than you is an idiot, and anyone going faster than you is a maniac?"
(George Carlin)

❧❧❧

"I have a flat tire. I should have brought asparagus!" (Anon)

⸎⸎⸎⸎

*"Always borrow money from a pessimist...
He won't expect it back!"*
(Oscar Wilde)

⸎⸎⸎⸎

"I doubt, therefore... I might be!" *(Anon)*

⸎⸎⸎⸎

*"If you try to fail and succeed...
which have you done?"*
(George Carlin)

⸎⸎⸎⸎

*"People say nothing is impossible,
yet I do nothing every day."*
(A.A. Milne)

⸎⸎⸎⸎

*"A diamond is merely a lump of coal
that did well under pressure."*
(Anon)

⌘⌘⌘

*"Even if you're on the right track, you'll
get run over if you just sit there."*
(Will Rogers)

⌘⌘⌘

*"Failure to plan on <u>your</u> part, does not
constitute an emergency
on <u>my</u> part."*
(Melanie Blankenship)

⌘⌘⌘

*"When we talk to God, we're praying.
When God talks to us...
we're schizophrenic."*
(Jane Wagner)

⌘⌘⌘

"If you think you are too small to make a difference,
try sleeping with a mosquito!"
(Dalai Lama)

❦❦❦

"When I was a boy,
the Dead Sea was only sick!"
(George Burns)

❦❦❦

"Two melons, who were deeply in love,
asked me one day what they should do,
since they were both anxious to get married,
but both sets of parents wanted to wait
and have a big wedding.
'Well then,' I replied quite wisely,
'You certainly cantaloupe!'"

❦❦❦

"Don't worry about the world
coming to an end tomorrow...
it's already <u>tomorrow</u> in Australia!"
(Charles Schultz)

❦❦❦

"Before you marry a person, you should
first make them use a computer
with slow Internet...
to see who they really are!"
(Will Ferrell)

❦❦❦

"I wonder why they call someone crazy, if they are seen performing for an invisible audience? Hey, at least they're working!"

❧❧❧

"I want my children to have all the things that I couldn't afford... then I want to move in with them!"
(Phyllis Diller)

❧❧❧

"At least... I still get paid!"
(Kathleen Scott-Kay)

❧❧❧

"My mother used to say, 'The older you get, the better you get... unless you're a banana.'"
(Betty White)

❧❧❧

"You know you've reached middle age when you're cautioned to slow down by your doctor, instead of by the police."

(Joan Rivers)

❧❧❧❧

"While in college, I argued that it is <u>literally impossible</u> to write a completely original song cycle! My composition teacher agreed...
So, I proceeded to compose,
'The Beatles Greatest Hits!'"

❧❧❧❧

"It took me fifteen years to discover I had no talent for writing, but I couldn't give it up... because by then I was too famous!"

(Robert Benchley)

❧❧❧❧

"Pulling my stomach in... depresses me!'"

❧❧❧❧

"I don't care what you think about me.
I don't think about you at all!"
(Anon)

❧❧❧

"If you want your children to be intelligent,
read them fairy tales. If you want them to be
more intelligent... read them <u>more</u> fairy tales!"
(Albert Einstein)

❧❧❧

"<u>Wife:</u> (sweetly) I've read that in some cultures,
when they die, people only list the
years on their tombstones when
they lived happily.
<u>Husband:</u> (sarcastically) Sounds good to me...
Be sure to write on mine...
'My husband was born dead!'"
(Anon)
(Shared by Natalia Todorov)

❧❧❧

"There is a silver lining in every tough situation.
I suggest taking that silver lining and
turning it in for cash!"

⁂

"Whenever people agree with me,
I feel that I must be wrong!"
(Oscar Wilde)

⁂

"When you failed at being nice,
you actually succeeded at being mean.
Success is everywhere, if you just know
where to look for it!"
(Katina Ferguson)

⁂

"If you pray for rain...
don't complain about the mud!"
(Hyacinth Mottley)

⁂

213

"Sometimes the reason the grass is always greener on the other side... is because it's fake!" (Anon)

(Shared by Linda Atherton)

"I didn't give you the finger. You earned it!"
(Bill Murray)

∞∞∞∞

"The holiday season doesn't need to be a nightmare of slowly driving through thick traffic, no parking spaces, overspending and long lines at the stores, but hey... It's tradition!"

∞∞∞∞

"We are taught in school that there is no such thing, as a __bad idea__. The creators of this belief have obviously never seen middle-aged men prancing around the beach in Speedos!"

∞∞∞∞

"Don't you think a stitch in time could be best achieved using a sewing machine?"
(Doug Kuhl)

∞∞∞∞

"I don't trust children.
They're here to replace us!"
(Stephen Colbert)

∽✺∽✺∽✺∽

"If first you don't succeed… just say you did!"

∽✺∽✺∽✺∽

"I started out with nothing…
and by golly, I still have most of it left!"
(Anon)

∽✺∽✺∽✺∽

"Opportunity does not knock… It presents
itself when you beat down the door!"
(Kyle Chandler)

∽✺∽✺∽✺∽

"Electricity… is just organized lightning!"
(George Carlin)

∽✺∽✺∽✺∽

"I finally realized that people are prisoners of their phones. That's why it's called... a 'cell' phone." (Anon)

❦❦❦

"I don't really believe I can make myself happy through the attainment of material things... but it's definitely worth a try!" (Anon)

❦❦❦

"The secret of staying young is to live honestly, eat slowly... and lie about your age!" (Lucille Ball)

❦❦❦

"As a child my family's menu consisted of two choices: take it or leave it." (Buddy Hacket)

❦❦❦

"If you cannot get rid of the family skeleton,
you may as well make it dance!"
(George Bernard Shaw)

❧❧❧❧

"How do you know if a cat
comes from a broken home?
Sadly, they don't have ma's...
only paws."

❧❧❧❧

"Here's a fun party game!
Have you ever tried to
kiss yourself on the cheek?"

❧❧❧❧

"By working faithfully eight hours a day,
you may eventually get to be boss...
and work twelve hours a day!"
(Robert Frost)

❧❧❧❧

"If you're going through Hell...
keep going!"

(Sir Winston Churchill)

"I've got a very clean conscience...
I haven't used it once!"
(Anon)

ഛഝഛഝ

"Ask not if the noble career you've
chosen is lucrative... ask if
there's a possibility of <u>jail time</u>!"

ഛഝഛഝ

"If you love two people at the same time,
pick the second one, because if
you really loved the first one...
you would never have
fallen for the second!"
(Johnny Depp)

ഛഝഛഝ

"Worrying is like paying a debt you don't owe!"
(Mark Twain)

ഛഝഛഝ

"The hardest years in life are those between ten and seventy."

(Helen Hayes)

⸎⸎⸎

"I love helpful advice. I only wish it came with instructions on how to achieve something... without doing anything!"

⸎⸎⸎

"Maybe if we tell people that the brain is an app... they'll start using it?" (Anon)

⸎⸎⸎

"A chicken in a field was curiously wailing, 'Moo,' along with all of the cows. Confused, I asked, 'Why are you mooing?' It replied, 'I am mooing because, clucking isn't considered PC anymore... and I find <u>oink</u>... just a wee bit beneath me.'"

⸎⸎⸎

"Life is a shipwreck... but we must not forget to sing in the lifeboats!"
(Voltaire)

෴

"I love mornings... I just wish they were in the afternoon!"
(Doug Kuhl)

෴

"Always remember, that you are unique... just like everybody else." (Anon)

෴

"You should never feel the need to call someone <u>a cheater, ugly and stupid</u> as the result of losing a game to them. That would be poor sportsmanship and so very immature. Anyway... I'm pretty sure they already know!"

෴

"Get your facts first, then you can distort them as you please!" (Mark Twain)

⚜⚜⚜

"Does seven days without meat... make one week?" (Anon)

⚜⚜⚜

"Don't tell me what to do! Only my wife can do that!"

⚜⚜⚜

"Never allow yourself to sit around unmotivated and uncertain of what to do next. Listen to that calm voice inside your head. It always has a great idea for you. It won't let up, either. In fact, sometimes...'It can be a real nag!'"

⚜⚜⚜

"Revenge is better than chocolate!" (Kurt Nielsen)

⚜⚜⚜

"I know when people speak the truth,
because when they do...
I always seem to agree with them!"

❦❧❦❧

"I understand that when life gives us lemons,
we should make lemonade... but what
about when it gives us eggplant?"

❦❧❦❧

"An Optimist: Someone who figures that
taking a step backward after taking a step
forward is not a disaster... it's a cha cha!"
(Anon)   (Shared by Douglas Newton)

❦❧❦❧

"My definition of an intellectual, is someone
who can listen to the 'William Tell Overture'
without thinking of the Lone Ranger."
(Billy Connolly)

❦❧❦❧

"I remember the time I was kidnapped and they sent a piece of my finger to my father. He said he wanted more proof!"
(Rodney Dangerfield)

⁓⌀⁓⌀⁓

*"When a husband is silent,
then he is a thinker.
When the wife is silent...
the thinker is in trouble!"*
(Natalia Todorov)

⁓⌀⁓⌀⁓

"If we didn't see it happen then how do we know that parts of our history have not been 'doctored' or made-up to represent what our leaders want us to believe? That answer is easy, because everyone knows... politicians don't lie!"

⁓⌀⁓

"If one door closes and another door opens...
your house is probably haunted!"

(Anon)

"It's even harder for the average ape to believe that he has descended from man!"
(H. L. Mencken)

⚜⚜⚜

"I always tell the truth! Sometimes it's just a little hard to find it... amongst all the lies."

⚜⚜⚜

"The best thing to do when you find yourself in a tight spot... is to lose a little weight!"

⚜⚜⚜

"Light travels faster than sound. This is why some people appear bright... until you hear them speak!"
(Alan Dundes)

⚜⚜⚜

*"If I were two-faced, would I
still be wearing this one?"*
(Abraham Lincoln)

⌘⌘⌘

*"When I was a kid my parents moved
a lot... but I always found them."*
(Rodney Dangerfield)

⌘⌘⌘

*"When people say unkind
things behind your back...
it's probably because your
front was too busy!"*

⌘⌘⌘

*"Never argue with stupid people.
They will drag you down to their level...
and then beat you with experience!"*
(Mark Twain)

⌘⌘⌘

"They say marriages are made in Heaven.
But so are thunder and lightning!"
(Clint Eastwood)

❦❦❦

"True terror is to wake up one morning and
discover that your high school class
is running the country!"
(Kurt Vonnegut)

❦❦❦

"The main difference between a
good-looking person and
a really 'hot' one...
is the sweat!"

❦❦❦

"I haven't spoken to my wife in years.
I didn't want to interrupt her."
(Rodney Dangerfield)

❦❦❦

"Can you tell time?
Good. Tell him that I'll be late!"

❧❧❧

"Friends are overrated. Remember,
if you are standing alone in a room,
you are automatically the smartest,
best looking, funniest, most creative
and most likeable person there!
How cool is that!"

❧❧❧

"If a man states an opinion and
there is no woman to hear it...
is he still wrong?" (Anon)

❧❧❧

"Carrots increase your vision...
alcohol doubles it." (Anon)
(Shared by Susan Elias)

❧❧❧

"I'm in shape. Round is a shape!" *(George Carlin)*

⸎⸎⸎

"Insanity runs in my family.
It practically gallops!"
(Cary Grant)

⸎⸎⸎

"A celebrity is any well-known TV or movie
star who looks like they spend
more than two hours...
working on their hair."
(Steve Martin)

✆✆✆✆

"I saw a guy at Starbuck's today. No iphone,
no tablet, no laptop. He just sat there.
Drinking coffee. Like a psychopath!"
(Kim Godby)
(Shared by Linda Atherton)

✆✆✆✆

"Here's all you have to know about men
and women: women are crazy, men
are stupid. And the main reason
women are crazy...
is that men are stupid!"
(George Carlin)

✆✆✆✆

*"My one regret in life is that
I am not someone else."*
(Woody Allen)

∽∝∽∝∽

*"A person who only believes in straight lines
and neat letters... will never be able
to read my handwriting!"*

∽∝∽∝∽

*"It's a well-known fact that
tall people are evil."*
(Kevin Hart)

∽∝∽∝∽

*"Sometimes, when I am in a situation where
I have no idea how to respond, I just take
a deep breath, plaster on my biggest smile
and say, 'What the hoodlehay!'"*
(Linda Atherton)

∽∝∽∝∽

Wise Italian saying:

"If you're a bear in the woods...
you'd better get ta some clothes on!"

❧❧❧

"You can lead a man to congress...
but you can't make him think!"
(Milton Berle)

❧❧❧

"I like women. I don't understand
them... but I like them."
(Sean Connery)

❧❧❧

"People often say that motivation
doesn't last.
Well, neither does bathing –
that's why we recommend it daily."
(Zig Ziglar)

❧❧❧

*"If money doesn't grow on trees, then
why do banks have branches?"*
(Anon)

⚬⚬⚬⚬⚬

"Are iphone chargers called apple juice?"
(Anon)

⚬⚬⚬⚬⚬

*"Never put off until tomorrow what you
can do the day after tomorrow."*
(Mark Twain)

⚬⚬⚬⚬⚬

*"Do you ever laugh, I mean, just howl at your
old pictures because you were so funny
looking in them? I do... I sometimes
crack-up for hours, nearly busting
a gut laughing at YOUR old pictures...
and your new ones too!"*

⚬⚬⚬⚬⚬

"I have the body of a God!"
(Unfortunately, it's Buddha!)
(Chris Breyer)

ᑲᑕᑲᑕ

"Be yourself; everyone else is already taken."
(Oscar Wilde)

ᑲᑕᑲᑕ

"There is not a better fragrance than
the sweet smell of success...
unless, of course, you prefer garlic."

ᑲᑕᑲᑕ

"When you are courting a nice girl,
an hour seems like a second.
When you sit on a red-hot cinder,
a second seems... like an hour!
That's relativity."
(Albert Einstein)

ᑲᑕᑲᑕ

"If we were on a sinking ship, and there was only one life vest... I would miss you so much!" (Anon)

"This is my step ladder.
I never knew my real ladder."
(Anon)

⁓⁓⁓⁓

"I always wanted to be somebody, but now I
realize I should have been more specific."
(Lily Tomlin)

⁓⁓⁓⁓

"Life is like a sewer... what you get out
of it... depends on what you put into it."
(Tom Lehrer)

⁓⁓⁓⁓

The bickering couple's motto:
"You have the right to remain silent!
Whatever you say can and will be
used against you!" (Anon)
(Shared by Stephen Murray)

⁓⁓⁓⁓

"If your friends __never__ disagree with you...
they're probably all imaginary!"

⌒⌒⌒⌒

"My mama always said,
what goes around comes around,
what goes up must come down,
everything in the dark must come to light
and if you eat too many sweets...
your teeth will fall out and you'll get fat!"
(Anon & Adapted)
(Shared by Tassa Hampton-Varga)

⌒⌒⌒⌒

"Sometimes you meet someone and you
know from the first moment, that you
want to spend your whole life...
__without__ them."
(Anon)
(Shared by Douglas Newton)

⌒⌒⌒⌒

"Someone stole my toilet! The police have nothing to go on." *(Anon)*

᪢᪢᪢

"Do not be so open-minded that your brains fall out."
(G.K. Chesterton)
(Shared by Linda Atherton)

᪢᪢᪢

"Some people are like clouds... When they disappear, it's a beautiful day." *(Anon)*

᪢᪢᪢

"Why do people say age is only a number? It's clearly a word." *(Anon)*

᪢᪢᪢

"Good friends don't let you do stupid things... unless they are invited along to partake!" *(Anon)*

᪢᪢᪢

"My brain handles getting older just fine...
it's my body that keeps protesting!"
(Anon)

✐✐✐

"I went to the air and space museum...
but there was nothing there." (Anon)

✐✐✐

"It's sad to me, how some people's great
talents or achievements are overlooked,
merely because they aren't deemed
popular. I daresay, in a hundred years,
long after the current 'popular' people
are dead and gone, we'll still be using
toilets, whether or not people know the
name of one of the <u>most prolific</u>
<u>builders and sellers</u> of toilets
in history! Three cheers for...
Mr. Thomas Crapper!"

✐✐✐

"No one has the right to tell me what to do...
except for my pastor, my boss, my fortune
teller, the police, the DMV, the IRS,
my doctor, my dentist, my yoga coach,
my bank, my creditors, my spouse,
my kids, the government...
Never mind."

❧❧❧

"As you get older, you've got to stay
positive. For example, the other day
I fell down the stairs. Instead of getting
upset, I just thought, 'Wow, that's the
fastest I've moved in years!'"
(Anon)
(Shared by Linda Atherton)

❧❧❧

"Where there's a will... there's a relative!"
(Ricky Gervais)

❧❧❧

*"Let's say that you want to fit-in with the in-crowd,
but you are NOT exceptionally funny, good looking,
rich or smart. No problem. Just be yourself!
No... Wait... That's not it?"*

⤖⤖⤖

243

*"If someone asks you if you want to order a pizza...
the correct answer will always be, 'Yes!'"*
(Katie Willert)

⌘⌘⌘

*"I'm gonna work on being less
condescending. (Condescending
means to talk down to people.)*
(Douglas Newton)

⌘⌘⌘

*"Speaking for myself, it's much more
palatable to discuss a problem together,
than to just be told what to do.
It makes me feel that my intellect
and experience are respected,
as well they should be...
Ooh! I hope my parents
invite 'Barney' to my
birthday party!"*

⌘⌘⌘

"This morning I saw a neighbor talking to her cat. It was obvious that she thought her cat understood her. I told my dog... and we laughed a lot about it!"
(Natalia Todorov)

❧❧❧

"Never assume that everyone around you is exactly like you are... unless, of course, you are surrounded by mirrors."

❧❧❧

"No matter the situation, you can't be sad when you're holding a cupcake."
(Anon)

❧❧❧

"The best way to teach your kids about taxes, is by eating 30% of their ice cream!"
(Bill Murray)

❧❧❧

"The skunk smells itself first!"
(Anon)

❦❦❦

"I don't instantly make a distorted facial expression or shout something disapproving when I am first meeting people, and detect a 'foul stench' in the air, because, actually, I am deeply in thought... trying desperately to figure out a way to 'politely' shift the blame!"

❦❦❦

"One of the most striking differences between a cat and a lie, is that a cat only has nine lives."
(Mark Twain)

❦❦❦

"My wife and I were happy for twenty years... and then we met." *(Rodney Dangerfield)*

❦❦❦

"I was planning on going to the gym...
but I got a better offer from
my refrigerator!"
(Melanie Bowles-Azpeitia)

⁂

"Some people are just born funny!
It's the outrageous things they
say, that makes us laugh,
almost <u>every</u> time they speak!
That's politicians for you!"

⁂

"Attracting little praise from others, doesn't
necessarily mean you have gone completely
unappreciated. It may be that on those rare
occasions when other people actually <u>see</u>
you working... they are <u>so</u> impressed,
that they are left utterly speechless!
But probably not."

⁂

**"Common sense is not a gift!
it's a punishment, because you
have to deal with everyone
who doesn't have it!"**
(Anon)
(Shared by Vincent Washington)

ᑲᑯᑲᑯᑲᑯ

**"You have to be 100% behind someone...
before you can stab them in the back."**
(Ricky Gervais)

ᑲᑯᑲᑯᑲᑯ

**"Stressed, spelled backwards is 'desserts.'
Coincidence? I think not!"** *(Anon)*

ᑲᑯᑲᑯᑲᑯ

**"If you think nothing is impossible...
try slamming a revolving door!"**
(Anon)

ᑲᑯᑲᑯᑲᑯ

*"I asked for a pound of ladyfingers
at the supermarket.
So, the lady stocking the shelves...
<u>punched</u> me!"*

"I don't really attend funerals that start before noon. I guess I'm not a 'mourning' person."

(Anon)

⌘⌘⌘

Taking a dog named, Shark, to the beach... is a bad idea."

(Anon)

(Shared by Natalia Todorov)

⌘⌘⌘

"I Leave my house a mess, so when my friends visit... they go home feeling <u>better</u> about their own housekeeping skills. I'm that good of a friend!"

(Anon)

(Shared by Cheri Martinson)

⌘⌘⌘

"Having a sister is like

having a parasite.

You're attached to her for life!"

(Haylie James)

❧❧❧

"If you can't live without me,

why aren't you dead already?"

(Cynthia Heimel)

❧❧❧

"If money is the root of all evil...

then why doesn't it grow into

evil things when I plant it?"

❧❧❧

"I thought the dryer made my clothes shrink.

Turns out it was the refrigerator."

(Anon)

(Shared by Elizabeth Garcia)

❧❧❧

"An evil queen on her death bed, called her errant son to her side, and told him, 'Upon my death I bequeath you the kingdom of Nada.' The prince looked at her strangely and replied, 'But there is no kingdom of Nada?' The queen smiled cruelly, and quickly retorted, 'And there is no inheritance for you, either, you rogue, breaker of laws and pub-hopper!' Showing no signs of shock, anger or disappointment, the prince replied calmly, "I am just like you!" The queen reared back in hatred, unleashing one hideous word, in hopes of crushing the prince, "Dog!" The prince regally bowed his head, smiled respectfully, and replied politely, 'Bitch!'"

ઝ૭ઝ૭ઝ૭

"Why did the Frenchman run inside the restaurant and straight through to the back, without sitting down at a table? Because he had to 'oui oui.'"

ઝ૭ઝ૭ઝ૭

"I'm not afraid of death. I just don't want to be there when it happens!"
(Woody Allen)

∽∾∽∾∽

"Excuse me... do you have the thyme?"
(Anon)

∽∾∽∾∽

"I love animals... they're delicious."
(Anon)
(Shared by Doug Kuhl)

∽∾∽∾∽

"Political correctness is tyranny with manners."
(Charlton Heston)

∽∾∽∾∽

"Be careful when you follow the Masses.
Sometimes the 'M' is silent!" *(Anon)*

∽∾∽∾∽

"Cheese is the 'gratest' thing I know!"

⌘⌘⌘

"Forgive your enemies...
but never forget their names!"
(John F. Kennedy)

⌘⌘⌘

"Starting tomorrow, whatever life throws at me...
I'm ducking so it hits someone else!" *(Anon)*
(Shared by Patricia Mountain-Romero)

⌘⌘⌘

"If I give you a straw will you go suck the
fun out of someone else's day?"
(Anon)

⌘⌘⌘

"Never go to bed mad... Stay up and fight!"
(Phyllis Diller)

⌘⌘⌘

"Look out for number one...

and don't <u>step</u> in number two!"

(Rodney Dangerfield)

(Shared by Annette Ambrose-Schumann)

"Why is Miss Universe always from Earth?"
(Anon)
(Shared by Laura Ann Washington-Franklin)

⸺⸻⸺

"Anyone who lives within their means,
suffers from a lack of imagination."
(Oscar Wilde)

⸺⸻⸺

"Nothing spoils a good story
like the arrival of an eyewitness."
(Mark Twain)

⸺⸻⸺

"If all else fails... follow directions!"
(Robert Willert)

⸺⸻⸺

"When nothing goes right... go left!" (Anon)

⸺⸻⸺

"I spilled spot remover on my dog.
He's gone now."
(Steven Wright)

⸎⸎⸎

"You can't have everything...
Where would you put it?"
(Anon)

⸎⸎⸎

"Housework can't kill you...
But why take a chance?"
(Phyllis Diller)

⸎⸎⸎

"We gotta start thinking about the world
we'll leave behind for Betty White
when we're all gone." (Anon)
(Shared by Douglas Newton)

⸎⸎⸎

"Having a smoking section in a restaurant,
is like having a peeing section
in a pool!"
(Bill Murray)

"To make a mistake is human, but to blame it
on someone else... is even more human."
(Anon)

"I intend to live forever. So far, so good!"
(Steven Wright)

"If Satan ever lost his hair...
there would be hell toupee!"
(Anon)
(Shared by Linda Atherton)

"Common sense is like deodorant.
The people who need it
most... never use it!"
(Anon)

⬥⬥⬥⬥

"My decision-making skills closely
resemble that of a squirrel...
when crossing the street."
(Anon)

⬥⬥⬥⬥

"Time is precious... Waste it wisely!"
(Anon)

⬥⬥⬥⬥

"I asked my brother if he knew anything
about earwax?
He nodded, with a smile...
and then whacked my ears!"

⬥⬥⬥⬥

"I tried to catch some fog... I mist."

(Anon)

❧❧❧

"Seeing a spider in my room isn't scary.
It's scary when it disappears."

(Anon)

❧❧❧

"Why did the blonde stare at a frozen
orange juice can for 2 hours?
Because it said, 'Concentrate!'"

(Anon)

❧❧❧

"Politicians and diapers must
be changed often...
and for the same reason!"

(Mark Twain)
(Shared by Douglas Newton)

❧❧❧

"Humor is just another defense against the universe!"
(Mel Brooks)

⸎⸎⸎

"My wife yelled from upstairs and asked, 'Do you ever get a shooting pain across your body, like someone's got a voodoo doll of you and they're stabbing it?' Sounding concerned, I replied, 'No...' She responded, 'How about now?'"
(Anon)
(Shared by Chris Breyer)

⸎⸎⸎

"When you are dead, you do not know you are dead. It's only painful and difficult for others. The same applies when you are stupid."
(Ricky Gervais)

⸎⸎⸎

EPILOGUE

Writing and collecting all of the motivational sayings in this book involved a great deal of time, a great many people and a great amount of inspiration. After completing the writing of this book, I think everyone involved with the project better understands that creating a motivational saying is much easier when you have a personal experience... **or a current-event to base part of it on.**

We were writing this book over the exact months (December 2019 – April 2020) that the corona virus (COVID 19) pandemic was first being discussed and later when it began sweeping the world, giving us plenty to inspire us as the story unfolded. Most of our sayings, concerning this pandemic, involve *kindness, working together* and *keeping a positive attitude.* Thankfully, those of us who wrote those sayings were clever enough that most people reading them would probably have little idea that they were strongly inspired by the pandemic at all, and could therefore, apply them more generally to other things, as they were so intended. At the time this book was completed and sent off to the publisher, the pandemic was still happening, and we were still dealing with social distancing and edicts directing most people to stay at home. But... the country was beginning to plan the 'reopening of life,' sometime in the not too far off future, so it felt to me like a major improvement was definitely just over the horizon, and in a reasonable time, this situation would be more under control. Here's hoping!

I also hope you enjoyed reading the diverse mixture of motivational thoughts and observations held in this book. They were written for all of us. If all the things in life we fear, were somehow eradicated from the Earth, one day, many of these sayings would not be so strikingly appropriate! But, until that time comes, read this book and others like it, just to remind yourself... *"No matter how tough things may get, you will always find strength and hope through the sharing of love... and the possession of a positive mindset!"*

God Bless,

Dave Willert

Illustrations
BY DOUG KUHL

www.ingramcontent.com/pod-product-compliance
Lightning Source LLC
Chambersburg PA
CBHW050619110426

42813CB00010B/2607